45 Conversations About Behavioral Economics

Li Way Lee · Aaron Keathley

45 Conversations About Behavioral Economics

An Interdisciplinary Discussion Crossing Business, Public Policy, Sociology, and Psychology

palgrave
macmillan

Li Way Lee
Department of Economics
Wayne State University
Detroit, MI, USA

Aaron Keathley
Department of Economics
Wayne State University
Detroit, MI, USA

ISBN 978-3-031-05045-9 ISBN 978-3-031-05046-6 (eBook)
https://doi.org/10.1007/978-3-031-05046-6

This Palgrave Macmillan imprint is published by the registered company Springer Nature Switzerland AG
The registered company address is: Gewerbestrasse 11, 6330 Cham, Switzerland

Preface

Imagine walking through a farmers market on a Saturday. Shoppers are roaming around, many in groups of two or more. Stores and peddlers are everywhere, handing out coupons, offering samples, advertising and selling. Soft music and sweet aromas fill the air. Guards in uniform (and plain cloth) cruise around. Scammers and raiders lurk around every dark corner.

Nothing in this market is fixed; everything evolves. This market is what we find in the real world. And this market is what we talk about in this book.

The conversational format is a distinguishing mark of this book. A good conversation is spontaneous, not formulaic. It is give-and-take, not monopolistic. The tones are natural, not soprano. A good conversation is not driven by ideologies, paradigms, models, and jargons. It is organic and cage-free.

Another distinguishing mark is that the conversations are intergenerational. The two of us are 54 years apart in age. We bring different mental frames and cultural perspectives. That gives us a lot to space to explore.

Rest assured, however, that all our conversations come in bite-size portions: each shall take no more than 20 minutes to digest.

Detroit, USA

Li Way Lee
Aaron Keathley

Acknowledgments

The conversations compiled here began in a class. During group discussion, ideas would get tossed around, some abandoned, and some adopted as wisdom of the crowd. We did not keep a full list of those ideas. Nevertheless, we acknowledge them all.

In that class, we read two books: Morris Altman's *Behavioral Economics for Dummies*, and Paddy Hirsch's *Man vs. Markets*. Both informed and inspired many of our conversations.

To the two reviewers of our book proposal, we say: Thank you, thank you; you will find your ideas throughout the book.

Contents

List of Figures

PART I

Supply

There are lots of firms. We face a choice right off the bat. Do we walk around the firms, or do we climb inside a few first and check them out? We choose to climb inside a few firms first.

Interestingly, the inside of a firm turns out to be a universe of networks. We talk about why a firm has these networks and what purpose each network serves.

When we climb out of firms, we find that they form networks also. We talk about the good, the bad, and the ugly of these interfirm networks.

Here is a map of our discussion about firms:

A. Networks in a Firm
B. Fragility
C. Complexity
D. Similarity
E. Networks among Firms
F. Externalities

(We have 15 conversations about firms.)

By the end of the tour in this part, you will have seen a live picture of supply that is bigger than the sum of its parts.

CONVERSATION 1

Networks in a Firm: Why Firms

Prompt One day in early 1930s, a British college student by the name of Ronald Coase boarded a ship bound for North America. He found his way to Ford and GM assembly plants in Michigan. There, he spent a year looking for an answer to the question that had been bugging him: If prices were so good at allocating resources—as all his professors were telling him—then why would there be so many foremen and managers who make their living by performing the same function? Why are there "…islands of conscious power in this ocean of unconscious operation like lumps of butter coagulating in a pail of butter milk?" (Robertson 1923, p. 84) Coase's answer, half of a century later, won him a Nobel Prize in economics. What is his answer?

Keathley: Ronald Coase's work that earned him the 1991 Nobel Prize in economics had to do with transaction costs. Transaction costs are costs of running a business. These are not the traditional production cost and transportation cost that firms incur, but rather the cost of managing a firm and executing contracts. Before Coase, "traditional basic microeconomic theory was incomplete because it only included production and transport costs, whereas it neglected the costs of entering into and executing contracts and managing organizations" (The Royal Swedish Academy of Sciences 1991).

L. W. Lee and A. Keathley, *45 Conversations About Behavioral Economics*, https://doi.org/10.1007/978-3-031-05046-6_1

This explains why there are so many foremen and supervisors in the workplace. These positions help to execute contracts and assure that the firm runs smoothly. The cost of contracting is the transaction cost. Without foremen and supervisors, the transactional aspects of the firm would be haphazard and inefficient. Firms need to have these people at various stages of carrying out a contract to confirm that things are proceeding as they should. At the end of the day, transaction costs explain why firms develop at all. If our world did not have transaction costs and the need for organization, everyone would do business solo. And the firm would not arise.

This also helps to understand why, as D.H. Roberson (p. 84) put it, firms are "islands of conscious power in this ocean of unconscious operation like lumps of butter coagulating in a pail of butter milk." In this metaphor, the economy as a whole is the pail of buttermilk. And the lumps of butter are organizations for executing transactions according to contracts. That is why there are firms.

Overall, Coase's work on transaction costs, alongside his work on property rights, was instrumental in deepening our understanding of the firm and the economic costs that it faces. It also helped to explain why certain jobs are common in firms, despite their non-obvious contribution to profits. His later work continued upon these ideas to discuss contracts and how transaction costs determine whether contracts occur or do not occur. Without Coase's work in these areas, it is impossible to understand the ideas of externalities and social costs.

Lee: Alright, you nailed the idea of transaction cost. It took me longer. I did not even hear about it until I was in graduate school. When I fully grasped it, I recorded how I did it in a paper (Lee 1987).

Take the case of an apple. What makes the apple grow on a farm and then move to your plate? (This is "resource allocation.") According to conventional wisdom, the mover is the price system: all the prices of apples, oranges, trips to Honolulu, shoes, car insurance, state sale taxes, your paycheck and so on and so forth. Seriously, slow down and let me tell you how I buy that apple. I look at the prices of apples, oranges, strawberries, and vegetables. Then I check that apple for bruises, worms, or signs of pesticides. Then I touch it to make sure it is not smashed. However, I can't see the inside. What if I find that the apple is after all rotten inside after I have paid for it and taken a bite of it? Would I—could I—bring it back for exchange or refund? Does the store have a customer service counter? What is the policy about refunding a partially eaten apple? What if the store refuses to do anything about it? Could I file a lawsuit against the store?

I don't need to stretch my imagination more to see that, by the time I take a bite at the apple, it is no longer that humble apple that just got picked off the tree. It has become a sophisticated apple. It has involved the drawing, monitoring, and enforcement of a library of implicit and explicit contracts. All these activities entail cost. Transaction cost, that is.

Now, let's see if we can explain why firms like Kroger come about. Supermarkets are emblematic of transaction cost. Kroger, I am sure, did not emerge just to bring groceries to your neighborhood. Famers and vendors can do that. Kroger emerged and you go to Kroger so you and Kroger can voluntarily carry out a transaction at the lowest cost. A successful store like Kroger makes transactions so easy that you don't even think about the implicit and explicit contracts that support them. Here is a mental experiment that sheds light on this point. Imagine that, just when you are about to enter Kroger to get apples, you see a guy sitting in a truck with a sign: "fresh apples, same price as Kroger's." Would you buy from this guy? Why not?

You know, Coase did not say that the price system is irrelevant; he said that it takes more than the price system for an apple to move from farm to your plate. For having said that, he became a renegade. That is how I explain why it took the economics profession half of a century to endorse him for a Nobel Prize. Meanwhile, he took refuge in law school, where he wrote other great stuff. He also managed to live 103 years.

References

Lee, Li Way. "The Coasian Firm." *Journal of Behavioral Economics*, Summer 1987, pp. 1–7.

Robertson, D. H. *The Control of Industry*, Harcourt, Brace and Company, New York, 1923.

The Royal Swedish Academy of Sciences. "The Sveriges Riksbank Prize in Economic Sciences in Memory of Alfred Nobel 1991: Ronald H. Coase." 15 October 1991: https://www.nobelprize.org/prizes/economic-sciences/1991/press-release/.

Further Readings

Coase, R. H. *The Firm, the Market, and the Law*, The University of Chicago Press, Chicago, 1988.

Lee, Timothy. "The Coase Theorem Is Widely Cited in Economics. Ronald Coase Hated It." *The Washington Post*, 4 September 2013: https://www.washingtonpost.com/news/wonk/wp/2013/09/04/the-coase-theorem-is-widely-cited-in-economics-ronald-coase-hated-it/.

Networks in a Firm: Gabrielle's Barber Shop

Prompt The barber shop at the local mall has 6 people working in there. One is the owner-and-manager Gabrielle. (Incidentally, Gabrielle does not do hair.) The other 5 people only do hair, each reporting to Gabrielle as the boss. Let's describe Gabrielle's barber shop in greater details:

a. Draw the network picture of this barber shop. (Hint: It is a star network.)
b. What are the average degrees of connection and separation of this network?

Keathley: Fig. 2.1 is what Gabrielle's barbershop looks like:

Figure 2.1 is a star network. Each peripheral node around the central one represents one of the barbers in the shop. Each barber is connected directly to the owner-manager Gabrielle. If they wish to interact with each other regarding, say, who will serve which customer, they go to Gabrielle. This allows each barber to spend the most amount of time on styling hair, rather than on trying to coordinate the assignment of clients.

I like to think of the network in Fig. 2.1 as similar to a network you have in your own home, the internet. In the star network, your router is the central node. It acts as the owner-manager and makes sure that each device or website in the network gets the information it needs. If you would like to watch a movie on your computer, the router takes

L. W. Lee and A. Keathley, *45 Conversations About Behavioral Economics*, https://doi.org/10.1007/978-3-031-05046-6_2

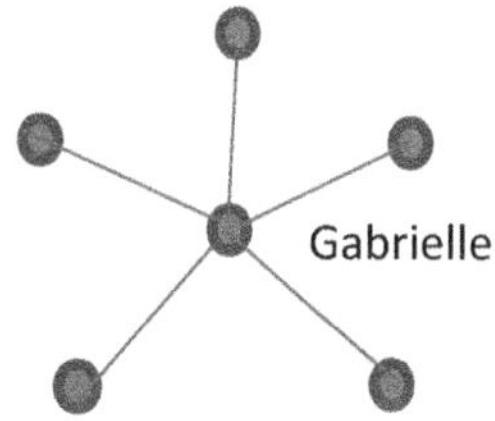

Fig. 2.1 A barber shop

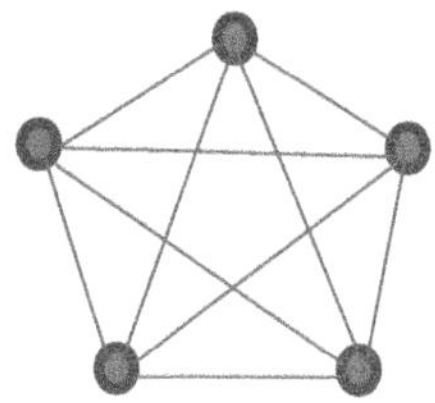

Fig. 2.2 A barber co-op

information from the first node (the computer) and gives it to the next node (the movie steaming service). When the movie streaming service node decides it needs to send out visual feedback to the user's request, it tells the router, and the router tells your computer. In any star network, the central node is the go between for any two peripheral nodes in the network.

This is optimal because the peripheral nodes are focused on their tasks and the central node handles all of the coordination and management. Each node is never more than one communication with the central node away from delivering information to whichever peripheral node it desires. As long as the central node is up to the task, I think this is a great way to organize a network in a firm with a defined owner-manager.

Lee: A beautiful diagram. I don't know how router works, but I am not surprised that a router is the central node of a star network. The router in my house has its own desk and I am always told to watch it when my laptop does funny things.

Let me use Fig. 2.1 to drive home a point: Gabrielle's profit is the saving in transaction cost that she makes possible. Imagine that, before Gabrielle came along, the five barbers formed a "co-op," as in Fig. 2.2. In this co-op, every member dealt with every other member. It is what is called a complete network. Take barber Derrick. He had to deal with the other four: Sudip, Morris, Kathleen, and Nancy. So Derrick had to manage 4 relations. Since this is true of everyone, and there were 5 people in the co-op, there were a total of $4 \times 5 = 20$ relations.

When Gabrielle showed up and took over as the owner-manager, the barber shop underwent a dramatic change. It became the star network in Fig. 2.1. In this new organization, there are only 5 links. Each link runs both ways: for example, Gabrielle needs to manage a relation with Derrick and Derrick needs to manage a relation with Gabrielle. So, there are a total of 10 relations to manage in the barber shop now.

Now the star network represents a saving of 10 relations, thanks to Gabrielle. If each relation costs $1000 a month to manage, regardless of who the parties are, then you can see where the saving comes from. This saving is equal to $1000 × 10, or $10,000. Gabrielle may or may not want to share the saving with the employee barbers. In any case, the employees will not be worse off, and Gabrielle can keep all the saving in transaction cost and call it "profit."

As you delve deeper into network theory, you will need to acquire new vocabulary like the average degree of connections and the average degree of separation. Have you ever heard of the phenomenon "Six Degrees of Separation" (Watts 2004)? We will talk about it later. Just for some fun now, let me offer my guess of the average degree of separation in Fig. 2.2: exactly 1.0. Run a check on it.

Reference

Watts, Duncan J. *Six Degrees: The Science of a Connected Age*, W. W. Norton, New York, NY, 2004.

Further Reading

Goyal, Sanjeev. *Connections: An Introduction to the Economics of Networks*, Princeton University Press, Princeton, NJ, 2007.

Networks in a Firm: Separation of Ownership and Control

Prompt At about the same time when Ronald Coase was trying to figure out why there are firms, Adolf Berle and Gardiner Means (1932) looked into firms and saw something alarming in the larger ones: ownership and control are separated from each other. (Let's call this phenomenon SOOC: separation of ownership and control.) Why did Berle and Means find SOOC alarming?

Keathley: Berle and Means were so alarmed by SOOC because they saw it as catastrophic for the shareholder. They believed that those who were managing the day-to-day operation of the firm would put their interests above those of the owners. They believed that SOOC was not good for shareholders and investors in the long term. It is easy to see how they came to this conclusion. Put yourself in the place of a manager at a factory, and your primary interest will not be to maximize profits for the shareholders. Berle and Means advocated for voting power for shareholders, increased transparency, and accountability. They did not like that the typical shareholder had become a passive owner: the owner simply had "exchanged the position of independent owner for one in which he may become merely recipient of the wages of capital" (Berle and Means 1932).

L. W. Lee and A. Keathley, *45 Conversations About Behavioral Economics*, https://doi.org/10.1007/978-3-031-05046-6_3

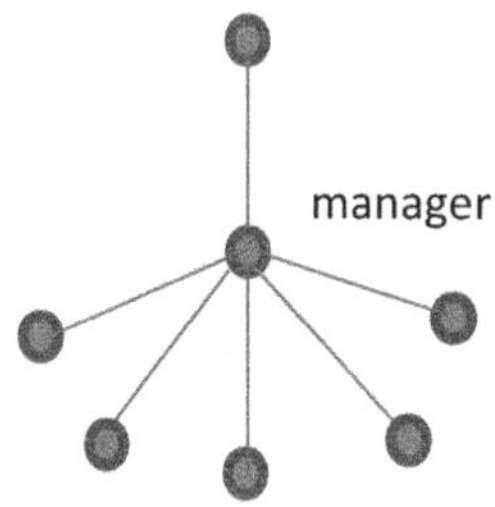

Fig. 3.1 A barber shop with separation of ownership and control

As an example, we can look at Gabrielle's barber shop in the earlier conversation. Suppose that, one day, Gabrielle gets fed up with dealing with disorderly employees and unhappy customers. So, she hires a professional manager, while she remains the owner. There are 7 people at the barber shop now. Figure 3.1 is the network that comes about. The central node is no longer Gabrielle, but the new manager. Gabrielle has become what Berle and Means talked about: a passive owner. She has no control over how the actual business is run; she only gets what is left at the end of the day: so-called profit. The true control of the business and its profit are in the hands of the new manager.

The manager pursues self-interest. Whatever it is, it is not profit. That is alarming because economic theory assumes that profit drives efficiency. When firms do not pursue profit anymore, the capitalistic economy may collapse. This is why Berle and Means were so concerned about SOOC.

Lee: I love Fig. 3.1. It is impossible to improve. So let me just expand on your story about it.

Let's go back to the barber shop and brainstorm about its past, present, and future. In an earlier conversation, we talked about the days of the barber shop when it was a co-op of five barbers. Then we talked about how they got tired of dealing with each other and went to Gabrielle to ask her to take over as the owner-and-manager. Gabrielle agreed. She would manage all the relations among employees, take care of customer complaints, pay all the bills, and keep for herself only what is left. That was a while ago. Fast forward to today. Gabrielle has turned 70; she feels the weight of all her responsibilities is growing. She fears that it is crushing her. What can she do? She faces three options:

- close the shop;
- downsize it by letting a few barbers go;
- hire someone to take over management.

Let's say Gabrielle hires Cindy to take over management. By doing so, Gabrielle separates ownership and control. Cindy is at the control center now, managing relations among the five barbers. Meanwhile, Gabrielle pays all bills for building, equipment, salaries of 6 people (5 barbers and Cindy), plumbing, cleaning, and utilities. Then, at the end of the day, Gabrielle takes home whatever is left after deducting the expenses from the revenue. If there is nothing left, then Gabrielle takes the loss all by herself.

Everything is going to be just fine, right? Well, not quite. Gabrielle has no reason to trust Cindy completely. She still has to keep an eye on Cindy. In fact, she tells Cindy that they will do weekly one-on-ones and quarterly performance reviews. The metric of performance is one singular thing: profit.

Both Gabrielle and Cindy know that profit is a poor metric for managerial performance. Profit depends on numerous variables out of the manager's control. The town may boom, following an influx of rich residents. Business picks up, driving up profit for Gabrielle. Or a pandemic may shut down all gyms, restaurants, and barber shops in town. Gabrielle suffers loss. These ups and downs in the economy are more powerful driving forces than Cindy's devotion and acumen as the manager. Gabrielle should not hold Cindy solely responsible for profit and loss. As people in business, they know that.

So, what do Gabrielle and Cindy do with the profit metric during performance review? We will have a conversation about it shortly. Next, we need to take notice of a further development related to SOOC.

Reference

Berle, Adolf A., and Gardiner C. Means. *The Modern Corporation and Private Property*, 1st edition, The Macmillan Company, New York, 1932 (Revised edition by Harcourt, Brace & World, Inc., New York, 1967).

Further Reading

Lee, Li Way. *Industrial Organization: Minds, Bodies, and Epidemics*, Palgrave Macmillan, Switzerland, 2019.

Networks in a Firm: Board of Directors

Prompt In large firms, the separation of ownership and control (SOOC) goes much further: Owners delegate the task of monitoring the manager to another group called "Board of Directors" (BOD). Let's do a couple of things:

a. Draw the network picture of a firm with BOD.
b. Look up the BOD of a big firm. Does the Chief Executive Officer (CEO) chair the BOD?

Do you see conflict of interest in the arrangement?

Keathley: Fig. 4.1 is a network picture of a big firm such as General Motors.

The CEO is the central node. The CEO also is the chair of the Board of Directors. I see conflict of interest on top of conflict of interest. The groups have different goals. The workers want to do as little work as possible for the highest wage, the Board of Directors wants to maximize profit for shareholders, and the CEO wants to remain in her high-salaried position. In addition, with the CEO doubling as the chair of the Board of Directors, it is in board members' best interest to stay on the good side of the CEO. The CEO is essentially watching herself. No matter the context, a system like this is bad for anyone other than the CEO.

L. W. Lee and A. Keathley, *45 Conversations About Behavioral Economics*, https://doi.org/10.1007/978-3-031-05046-6_4

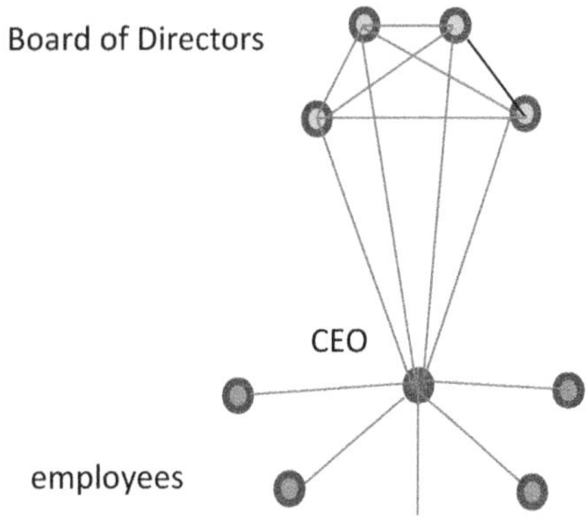

Fig. 4.1 A firm with a board of directors

The CEO's livelihood is tied to the immediate growth of the firm instead of the long-term health of the firm. This can help to explain a lot of risky decisions CEOs make in the modern world. The risk of over-leveraging your firm by expanding too quickly is smaller when you are your own oversight and you can pull the ripcord at any time.

Lee: Fig. 4.1 is a pretty picture! I see the BOD. (I also see a vacant employee position.) But where are the owners? Owners are supposed to be watching the BOD. Let's try Fig. 4.2.

Each node in Fig. 4.2 represents a group, which has its own network. So there are interlinked networks within a firm.

Like you, I see chock-full of conflict of interest in the boardroom of a corporation. Not the least of which is the CEO's serving as the chairperson of the BOD. There simply is something wrong about it.

Stepping back from the boardroom, I feel a bit better. A big firm today is nothing but a democracy. It has all these counterparts: citizens in shareholders, congress in BOD, and executive office in CEO. The details of democratic governance structures vary. As long as a democratic firm survives, its governance cannot be all that bad.

One other thing: The practice of having the CEO as chair of BOD is not universal. It seems to be more common in the U.S. than elsewhere. This has a calming effect on me.

Keathley: I agree with much of your comment, but not with the statement "As long as a democratic firm survives, its governance cannot be all that bad." Surely, we can hold ourselves to a higher standard than mere survival? Many nations have had democratic governance and still commit atrocities or have been inhumane. Perhaps I am an optimist, but I believe

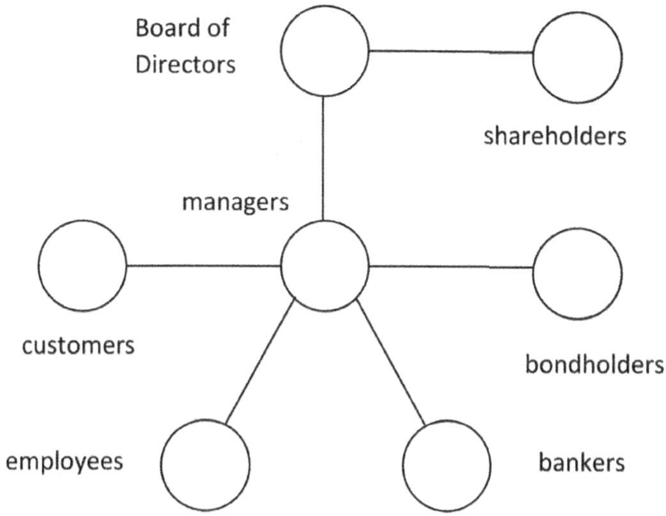

Fig. 4.2 Networks in a firm

that we can do better than letting those who have the most to gain be the ones who make the rules for firms.

Further Readings

Council on Foundations. "Should CEOs Be on the Board? And Should They Have Voting Rights?" 2010, accessed on 2 September 2021: https://www.cof.org/sites/default/files/documents/files/CEOs%20On%20Boards.pdf.

Macey, Jonathan R. *Corporate Governance: Promises Kept, Promises Broken*. Princeton University Press, Princeton, NJ, 2008.

Meredith, Patricia. *Better Boardrooms: Repairing Corporate Governance for the 21st Century*, University of Toronto Press, Toronto, Canada, 2020.

Fragility: The Urge to Build Empire

Prompt Managerial performance is a complex thing. We cannot measure it by profit, because profit depends on so many other micro and macro forces over which nobody has full control. Rather, we measure managerial performance by the firm's growth and market share. Call it "the growth heuristic." Let's talk about evidence of the growth heuristic. A good place to look is press releases. Let's see if the typical press release on a CEO uses the growth heuristic more often than the profit heuristic.

Keathley: I read a 2015 General Motors press release in search of evidence of the growth heuristic. I found several mentions about growth. CEO Mary Barra spoke about the different fields and areas that she expects General Motors to grow into. She also focused a lot on how the new things General Motors is working on would increase earnings per share and "generate significant shareholder value" (GM 2015). She did mention additional revenue and profit one time. She said that a car sharing program would have the capabilities to increase profit. However, talk of profit occurred much less frequently than talk of growth. This is a good example of the growth heuristic. At times, it seemed like she used growth as a blanket term for anything good.

As for market share, she did not mention it by name, but the entire press release was discussing how General Motors was expanding their portfolio of services offered. From car sharing to electric bikes to new fuel cell production, she made heavy mention of the new ways the General

L. W. Lee and A. Keathley, *45 Conversations About Behavioral Economics*, https://doi.org/10.1007/978-3-031-05046-6_5

Motors was looking to expand their reach into a myriad of markets. She finished her speech by again talking about growth, this time in quantifiable terms. She talked about how General Motors was aiming to grow over the next five years via a five billion dollar investment into growing the luxury family vehicle market. She briefly mentioned China and other areas of the globe that General Motors was looking to expand their influence into. Lastly, she made note of efforts to cancel out this increase in spending by improving cost efficiencies in certain areas of production.

Overall, this press release makes a great case for the growth heuristic. Rather than talking about profit or revenue for very long, Mary Borra chose to mention the ways that her firm would be growing the various aspects of its mix of products and services. Often the word growth was not needed to convey the message of expanding into new markets or increasing their presence in GM's existing markets.

Lee: I am surprised that it is GM's own press release. Great find! I am sure there are many reviews of Barra out there, and that she collects them all.

What does she learn from reviews of her as a CEO that she does not already know? Well, she learns how other people judge her and what the heuristics they use for judgment. She may find growth and market-share heuristics naïve and simplistic, but she can't change them. When she goes to her office, she will be sure to put mergers and acquisitions at the top of her agenda. She will want to grow GM in any way she can. Would a race car team count? Would a battery operation count? She will tell her VPs to get them. Never mind profitability. Just grow, grow, and grow.

Further, I think there is a feedback loop between growth heuristic and empire building:

- The more people use GM's growth to judge Barra, the more Barra wants to grow GM.
- The more GM grows, the more people use GM's growth to judge Barra.

Figure 5.1 is a snapshot of the loop.

A confession is in order. I am not that different when it comes to obsession with growth. Shortly after I had become a faculty member, I realized that my colleagues would judge me by my publications and not much else. I decided not to disappoint them. I would drive to my

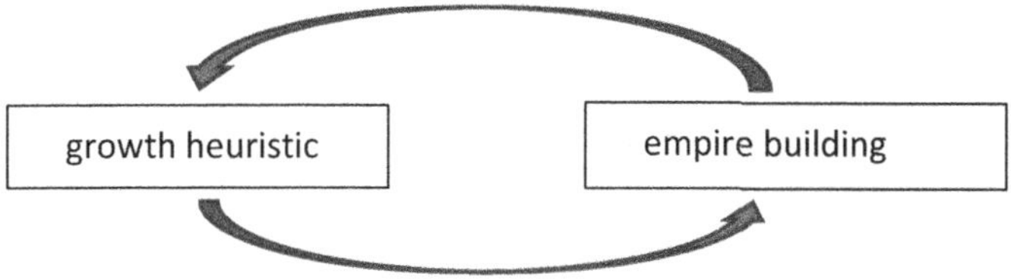

Fig. 5.1 Empire building

faculty office on weekends and holidays to do research. Did the parent in me think it was the best way to spend time? No, but the faculty in me thought it was. The faculty in me apparently was the better negotiator than the parent in me.

When it comes to making judgment about others, we all use heuristics. Try this thought experiment. You and your friend are standing in line for tickets to a basketball game. Your friend murmurs that one of the people in front of the line used to be the captain of the basketball team at her high school. You glance at the people in front of the line. What is the heuristic you use to pick out the captain? Don't tell me it is not height.

Reference

General Motors. "GM Outlines Plans to Capitalize on Future of Personal Mobility." *Media.gm.com*, 1 October 2015: https://media.gm.com/media/us/en/gm/news.detail.html/content/Pages/news/us/en/2015/oct/1001-gbc.html.

Further Reading

Robinson, Joe. "Is Your Managerial Ego Too Big?" *Entrepreneur.com*, 11 April 2014: https://www.nbcnews.com/id/wbna54928896.

CONVERSATION 6

Fragility: Leverage

Prompt During a financial crisis, our attention is drawn to a firm's leverage. Why do we care about leverage? What are the leverages of the largest 5 US banks these days?

Keathley: Banks are the grease that keeps economies running. In a scenario where banks all went bankrupt, the economy would be in shambles to a degree that the world has never seen before. When I say that banks are the grease of the economy, I mean that they are the institutions that enable businesses to carry out their financial transactions. Banks are used for loans to pay daily operations, survive a rough quarter, or get a quick jolt of cash to pay off debts. Also, banks are key to the lives of everyday individuals. We see time and time again in history that, when banks fail or people lose confidence in banks, bad things happen to everyone in the economy. In September and October 1929, the U.S. saw the stock market crash. People saw the market plummeting and went to empty their savings. (These are known as bank runs.) When lots of people withdraw all of their money from a bank at the same time, the bank is unable to fulfil these requests because it does not have enough cash on hand, and this leads the bank to fail. In more recent times, we have seen big banks like Lehman Brothers fail, and this bank failing contributed to the turning of a localized subprime mortgage crash into a global economic downturn. Simply put, when banks are failing, everyone gets hurt.

L. W. Lee and A. Keathley, *45 Conversations About Behavioral Economics*, https://doi.org/10.1007/978-3-031-05046-6_6

The top five banks in the U.S., in descending order of total assets, are: JP Morgan Chase, Bank of America, Wells Fargo, Citigroup, and US Bank. Their leverage ratios in the fourth quarter of 2019 are: 7.88%, 7.63%, 8.45%, 8.49%, and 8.18%, respectively. Leverage represents how much debt each bank has in relation to its total assets. For example, the largest bank, JP Morgan Chase has approximately 220 billion dollars in capital and 2.8 trillion dollars in leveraged debt. They have a debt ratio of 7.88%, this means that they have enough cash on hand to cover 7.88% percent of their debt at any time. At first this statistic was jarringly high, but then I researched the leverage of Lehman Brothers before it failed (Kaul 2018). They were leveraged in such a way that for every dollar that they had in assets, they had 30.70 dollars in outstanding debt. In other words, JP Morgan is in an infinitely better spot than Lehman Brothers was.

Lee: You have the right idea. But your terminology is loose and confusing. We need to fix that.

First, though, let me tell you a story about how I got to learn about leverage. When I was a graduate student, I spent days and nights studying the theory of the firm. The firm in textbooks is always wise and prudent, never taking too much risk or too little, always running with utmost efficiency, and always maximizing profit. Since I studied a lot in the Business School Library, I would occasionally glance at The Wall Street Journal. I noticed that, every day, some firms out in the real world were struggling or going bust. The stories were the same: The managers take too much risk, and don't give a hoot about profit. Wall Street—not just the journal—is a short subway ride from my school, so I couldn't very well ignore it. I started to experience cognitive dissonance. For the sake of my sanity, I decided to write my doctoral dissertation on corporate bankruptcy, something the textbooks never even touch on. That is how I learned about capital structure, debt-equity ratio, leverage, and all those ugly things in the guts of a firm.

Now, let's get back to terminology. Toss all those money-and-banking jargons that have crawled into our vocabulary. Instead, use the following list:

D	debt
E	equity
D + E	capital
D/E	debt-equity ratio
(D + E)/E	leverage (= debt-equity ratio + 1)

These five terms are all we need to talk about the fragility of a firm. In these terms, I can restate your finding about JP Morgan Chase as: "For example, the largest bank, JP Morgan Chase, has approximately 220 billion dollars in equity and 2.8 trillion dollars in debt... Its debt-equity ratio is 12.7 (2.8 trillion divided by 220 billion). Its leverage is 13.7 (12.7 plus 1)."

Leverage measures the fragility of a firm. It measures how many dollars of capital is riding on one dollar of equity. Leverage therefore gives you a sense of the shape of a firm. A firm with a low leverage has the structure of a pyramid; the firm can withstand shocks well. A firm with a high leverage has the structure of a pyramid on its head; it will easily topple over when the wind blows or the ground shakes. That is why, during financial crisis like that in 2008, the banks that failed all had high leverages. (One bank's leverage was close to 40. The bank's initials are D.B.) They also turned out to be the biggest banks. They were so big that the government could not risk their going bankrupt hand in hand and wrecking the entire economy. So the government bailed them out. Ever heard of those Too-Big-To-Fails?

References

Kaul, Vivek. "Explained: What Happened during the 2008 Lehman Crisis." *Mint*, 13 September 2018: www.livemint.com/Industry/Gi4CgVYJ4QLOiVGRKqx8JO/Learning-from-Lehman-what-goes-around.html.

Further Reading

BankRegData.com. "Tier 1 Leverage Ratio: All US Banks," accessed on 2 September 2021: www.bankregdata.com/allHMmet.asp?met=LEV.

Lee, Li Way. *Industrial Organization: Minds, Bodies, and Epidemics*, Palgrave Macmillan, Switzerland, 2019.

Fragility: Skin in the Game

Prompt Investment guru Warren Buffet thought company managers ought to have "skin in the game." What is that? How does it affect the fragility of a firm?

Keathley: To start off, let's define the phrase "skin in the game." It is used in everyday language to refer to something of value that can be gained or lost. For example, if a baseball player secretly bets a large sum of money on his next big game, he has skin in the game. Warren Buffet coined this term for the world of investment (Kenton 2021). He originally used this term to describe a situation in which professional managers purchased stock in the company that they were running. For example if the CEO of General Motors purchased a lot of General Motors stock, she would have skin in the game.

Having your skin in the business you run can be both a good and a bad thing. It is bad because you would have an unfair advantage in influencing the outcome. Imagine a CEO of a large company who has massive swaths of stock. If he knows that the company is about to go through a rough patch, he will likely sell off his stock, or if he thinks it will go up soon, he will double down and buy more. If this sounds like insider trading, you are on the right track. In modern firms, the CEO has a broad range of power that can impact the firm dramatically.

L. W. Lee and A. Keathley, *45 Conversations About Behavioral Economics*, https://doi.org/10.1007/978-3-031-05046-6_7

On the other hand, skin in the game can be good for the business. Factory workers who own company stock have skin in the company. They will want to work harder so that the stock price continues to rise, and they continue to make more money.

Overall, I see a CEO's having skin in the game as a largely negative thing. It tends to invite nefarious actions.

Lee: Interesting take on skin in the game! It makes perfect sense, too.

I share your concerns about CEO's having a lot of skin in the game. It does create moral hazards. I find irony in the fact that skin in the game is intended to reduce moral hazards. There is a tradeoff here.

Let's take a closer look at the tradeoff. When owners hand control over to the manager, they get the burden of management off their backs. But not quite all burden. Owners know that they still need to keep an eye on the manager, who is naturally inclined to pursue self-interest. Now, it is a burden to watch someone all the time. When there are several owners, there is the temptation among them to take free ride on each other. Aaron, would you please go to the afternoon meeting with the CEO by yourself? I am not feeling well today and may have to take a trip to my doctor's office.

How do owners reduce the burden of "manager watching"? Well, one way is to reduce the root of the problem by making the manager have skin in the game. In addition to cash bonus, give the manager a batch of company shares. In addition to cash in severance package, throw in a bundle of company shares. With these provisions, the manager becomes an owner and has less incentive to goof off and neglect the pursuit of profit. The skin in the game effectively grows into a person in the game. It is as if the manager has two selves now, who watch each other and negotiate about conflict of interest.

This goes to show that there is no such thing as free skin. Skin in the game has both benefit and cost.

Reference

Kenton, Will. "Skin in the Game." *Investopedia*, 13 July 2021: https://www.investopedia.com/terms/s/skininthegame.asp.

Further Readings

Lee, Li Way. *Industrial Organization: Minds, Bodies, and Epidemics*, Palgrave Macmillan, Switzerland, 2019.

O'Neill, Moira. "Does Your Fund Manager Have Skin in the Game?" *Financial Times*, 24 June 2021: https://www.ft.com/content/6a3a7697-cda0-4221-a6ac-892f5c78b660.

CONVERSATION 8

Complexity: Your Favorite Processed Food

Prompt Check into your refrigerator and pantry. What are (a) your favorite "processed" food item and (b) your favorite "soft" drink? For each, list the ingredients. Why do you not choose simpler food and drink? Are the reasons nutritional, cultural, or commercial?

Keathley: My favorite processed food item is the frozen beef and bean burrito by El Monterey. It is simple and quick to make, meaty and savory, and it provides a filling late-night snack. The ingredients are: Water, Enriched Wheat Flour (Enriched With Niacin, Reduced Iron, Thiamin Mononitrate, Riboflavin, Folic Acid), Beef, Beans, Vegetable Oil (Soybean, Canola, Palm, And/Or Corn Oil), Contains 2% Or Less Textured Vegetable Protein (Soy Flour, Caramel Color), Isolated Pea Product, Salt, Chili Pepper, Dough Conditioners (Yeast, Wheat Gluten, Sugar, Guar Gum, Food Starch, Sodium Metabisulfite), Spices, Flavor, Savory Flavor (Yeast Extract, Soy Sauce [Wheat, Soybeans, Salt], Maltodextrin, Lactic Acid, Calcium Lactate, Salt).

My favorite soft drink is Coca-Cola, specifically the Coke made in Mexico. The main difference between the Coke made in the U.S. and the Coke made in Mexico is that Mexican Coke substitutes cane sugar for the artificial sweeter, high fructose corn syrup. This makes the product softer, more natural, tastier, and more expensive. I do not drink pop very often, but out of any pop this is the one that I would choose. The ingredients are: carbonated water, sugar, caramel color, phosphoric acid, natural flavors, and caffeine.

L. W. Lee and A. Keathley, *45 Conversations About Behavioral Economics*, https://doi.org/10.1007/978-3-031-05046-6_8

I try to choose more natural and nutritious foods under normal circumstances. However, convenience and location influence my choice in food. For example, I drink the Mexican coke only when I am at a Mexican restaurant for a special occasion. That is the only time I can justify paying the markup for cane sugar on an already high margin item. In the case of the processed frozen burritos, I eat those when it is late at night and I am hungry from either having a light dinner or being very late. They are a simple, beefy comfort food that really hits the spot when you are in the mood for something salty and spicy.

I choose these foods over higher quality foods for different reasons. The Coke is like a wine or whiskey that couples have on their anniversary; it is for special occasions. Unless it is my birthday, paying $4 for a bottle of cola is absurd. The burritos come in on the other side of the spectrum. They are eaten for their convenience and availability at times when I don't have access to higher quality Mexican food.

Lee: You call that burrito simple food?! I don't know.

I have been obsessed with the question why modern food is so complex. After all these years, I have concluded that the answer lies in how we make choices in the face of complexity.

If we look at simple food like an apple, we will examine it for color, bruises, and aroma. The simplicity of an apple encourages us to gather information and use head to make decision. We do what is called *System-2 thinking* (Kahneman 2011). Now, when it comes to a box of cereal, we can't see or smell what is inside. So, we look at the picture on the box and the price. We may take a glance at the list of ingredients in small print, not expecting to understand all those chemical names. Then we decide whether to buy a box or not. After a few trips to the supermarket, we don't even look at the list of ingredients anymore. Just grab a box and move on to the next item on the shopping list. This way of making decision by impulse is called *System-1 thinking* (Kahneman 2011).

All the while, the sellers are taking notice. They will want to encourage System-1 thinking by kicking up the complexity of the cereal a notch. Figure 8.1 describes the feedback loop between the complexity of product and the simplicity of decision.

By itself, complexity is not a sufficient nudge. Take food, for example. Our taste for food has evolved to be what it is over hundreds of thousands of years. It is an instrument for survival. Things that are bad for

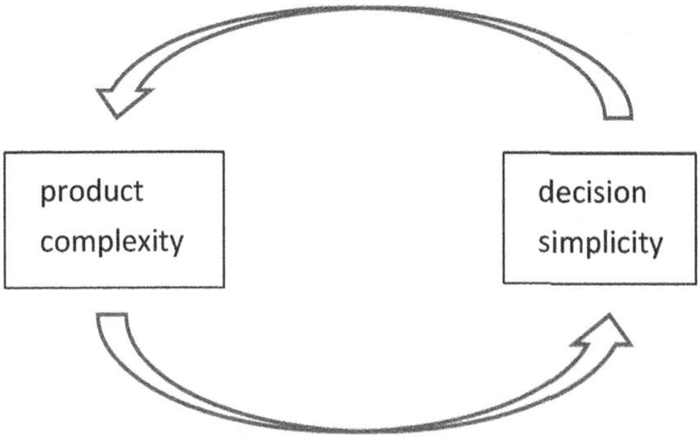

Fig. 8.1 The making of complex products

Fig. 8.2 How processed food comes about

health used to taste bad. Things that are good for health used to taste good. Taste is a System-1 heuristic. Today, producers are successful in making tasty complex food products. I will not say that complex food is necessarily junk food. We may talk about that link some other time. Here, I will say that food producers have hijacked our taste buds pretty well. Figure 8.2 tells my story.

Whatever the genesis of modern complexity is, complexity is an integral part of choice architecture. I find this idea most fascinating.

Reference

Kahneman, Daniel. *Thinking, Fast and Slow*, Farrar, Straus, and Giroux, New York, NY, 2011.

Further Readings

Arthur, W. Brian. *Complexity and the Economy*, Oxford University Press, 2015.
Colander, David, and Roland Kupers. *Complexity and the Art of Public Policy*, Princeton University Press, Princeton, NJ, 2014.

Complexity: The Complexity Fever

Prompt Once upon a time, General Motors sold many essentials of life: cars, home mortgage, checking account, saving account, auto insurance, home insurance, credit card. Find a few GM products today that surprise you.

Keathley: General Motors is an absolutely massive firm that has grown ferociously from where William Durant started it in 1908. They have over 100 years of business under their belt across all types of industries. They are obviously best known for their many brands of cars, but over the years they have produced many other goods and services. General Motors scientists were the inventors of the first mechanical heart pump (Parker 2020). They paved the way for all types of open heart surgeries. General Motors even donated this technology to our very own Wayne State University. General Motors was briefly in the train market (Parker 2020). They made trains from 1956 to 1966 and sold to places like Disney World and the Oregon Zoo. The last odd business venture by General Motors was a successful Australian racing team. Seeing a car business involved with racing isn't shocking, but this isn't a typical sponsorship deal. General Motors actually owns the entire team and it is one of the winningest teams in Australian racing history (Parker 2020).

General Motors currently produces houses for bats (Miller 2016). Yes you read "bats" correctly: the animal that flies. General Motors repurposes batteries from their Chevy Volt line of electric cars to create homes

L. W. Lee and A. Keathley, *45 Conversations About Behavioral Economics*, https://doi.org/10.1007/978-3-031-05046-6_9

for bats. General Motors also has entered the market for electric bikes. Not bikes as in motorcycles, but rather bikes as in bicycles. They launched this division in 2019 and are working on bikes that they plan to sell in urban environments. These bikes will be similar to the Bird scooters that I have seen in Detroit but will be fully fledged bicycles in shape and will be owned rather than rented. If you have a moment, give this a quick search, and look at them. The most interesting part about the design of one of the proposed models is that the bike folds completely in half for storage.

We've seen that General Motors has made some very interesting products throughout the years and we have barely even scratched the surface. I made no mention of their various financial services they offered over the years. It is easy to see how the modern large firm does much more than what they are commonly known for. Not all of these expansions have been successful, but for every failed train division you get one profitable bat house division.

Lee: GM is making electric bikes!? I did not know that. I will be on the lookout for them.

Here is a personal encounter with a conglomerate. It is common knowledge among folks of my age that, before GM collapsed in 2008, it had many automobile brands. In those days, I bought Oldsmobile Delta 88, Buick Park Avenue, Pontiac Bonneville, Buick Riviera, and Chevy Impala. Less known are the various GM financial products. I bought all my car insurance policies with GM Insurance. I had checking and saving accounts at the General Motors Acceptance Corporation. I also had home mortgage with GM's mortgage arm. You name it, GM had it, and I had it with GM. Oh, I left out my GM Mastercard.

GM stock back then was nothing but a complex financial derivative. Investors were investing in a conglomerate with car manufacturing, insurance, banking, lending, and mortgage.

By the way, I see a book project for you: *Empire Building: A History of GM*. I suggest that you organize the book by the four ways GM has tried to grow: horizontally, vertically, diagonally, and geographically.

- To grow horizontally, build plants and models (autos, bikes, whatever), merge with others, or acquire others.
- To grow vertically, there are two directions: upstream and downstream. In the upstream direction, buy or build battery plants for E-vehicles, E-bikes, E-boats, E-airplanes; and buy or build railroads

for moving parts and products. In the downstream direction, franchise more dealerships, build own dealerships, and offer loans and leases.

- To grow diagonally, build bat houses; buy racing teams; make organic sport drinks.
- To grow geographically, open dealerships in Antarctica, which is becoming warmer thanks to climate change; follow Tesla to Planet Moon.

References

Miller, Aaron. "Weirdly Surprising Things Car Companies Make, Besides Cars." Thrillist, 27 May 2016: www.thrillist.com/cars/nation/weird-things-car-manufacturers-make-besides-cars.

Parker, Garrett. "20 Fun Facts You Didn't Know About General Motors." Money Inc., 8 April 2020: moneyinc.com/20-things-didnt-know-general-motors/.

Further Reading

Amelunke, Joshua. "10 Major Car Companies That Make Other Things You Own." *Hotcars*, 9 June 2018: https://www.hotcars.com/car-companies-other-products/.

Lee, Li Way. *Industrial Organization: Minds, Bodies, and Epidemics*, Palgrave Macmillan, Switzerland, 2019.

Similarity: Models of Similarity

Prompt Two ice-cream stores are looking to establish themselves in a new town. They have the same ice-cream, and they have agreed to charge the same price and provide the same services. They are free to compete only in location. Consumers live in houses distributed uniformly in town. Where are the two stores going to be? Consider this in any of the following three scenarios:

(a) The town is a finite line.
(b) The town is a circle.
(c) The town is a disc.

Keathley: I remember this problem from a YouTube video that I watched years ago. I tracked down this video and re-watched it (de Haan 2012). Figure 10.1 sums up the video pretty well.

The video perfectly describes the line scenario. Imagine a beach one mile long, with swimmers evenly distributed. The first ice-cream cart sets up in the very middle of the beach. It serves every customer, who walks ½ of a mile at most. However, another ice-cream cart arrives the next day and the two carts decide to each stand one-quarter of a mile from each end of the beach and split the middle section of the beach. The video calls this the "socially optimal solution," since this requires the average consumer to travel the shortest distance. But this is not an equilibrium

L. W. Lee and A. Keathley, *45 Conversations About Behavioral Economics*, https://doi.org/10.1007/978-3-031-05046-6_10

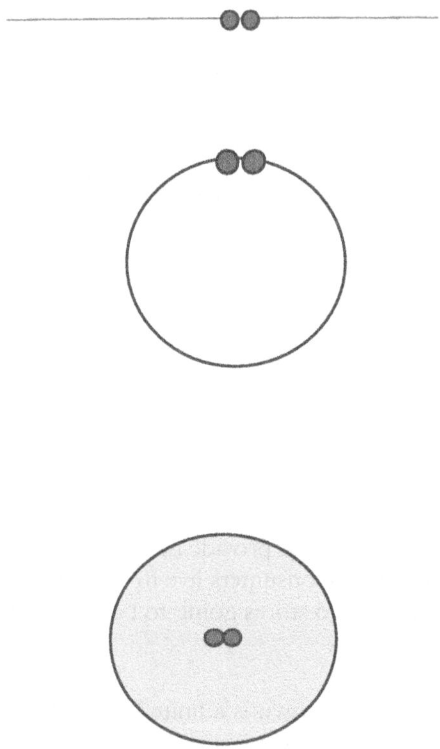

Fig. 10.1 Similarity in spatial competition

because each cart can sell more by moving toward the other. So the two carts will move toward each other until they are back-to-back at the center of the beach. Each cart serves exactly 50% of the customer base and if one cart moves away from the other cart at the center, it will only be surrendering customers. So, once at the center, neither cart will want to move away. Unfortunately, consumers are not doing as well as they could at the "socially optimal situation." Consumers on average walk 1/4 of a mile rather than 1/8 of a mile.

The circle scenario is a town with two ice-cream stores on it. (We will assume the middle of the circle is a lake or some zone where there can be no business.) In this town, no matter where the two stores sit, each store will get 50% of the population. Interestingly, a store cannot gain an advantage by moving closer to the other store. As one gets closer to the other, it gains on one side and loses on the other side. There are an infinite number of equilibriums. Welfare in this town is another matter. As with all of these situations the biggest loser is the consumer who is the farthest away from the nearest store. If the two stores decide to be next to each other, then some consumers have to travel half way around town.

The third scenario is a town that has the shape of a disc. I believe that we can expect the two stores to set up stores back-to-back at the center of the disc. In the beginning, there may have been only one store sitting at the center of disc. It would get 100% of the business. However, another store could move just next door. The two stores would start to poach on each other by moving around. Sooner or later both will settle down at the center, where neither business can undercut the other.

Lee: Good show of intuitive reasoning. I am a big fan of spatial models of competition. All of my thinking about competition is framed in terms of spatial models.

Keathley: Throughout writing and writing about spatial positioning, I wondered: how does this work out when stores are not easily movable? If a firm sets up a brick and mortar location, but is undercut spatially by another firm, what can they do to compete with this in the real world? It is very easy to move an ice-cream cart, but less easy to move a hardware store.

Lee: In that case, the store managers should watch that video and listen to our conversation before sinking money into ground. They should try to predict growth and decline of the population in this town, and future configuration of the town. They should also try to predict, for any population and each configuration of the town, how many stores are going to come into town and where the equilibrium configurations for the stores will be. For example, they may predict that a town will grow into a circle in a couple of years and it will have room for four stores. Then, what to do? For one thing, before breaking ground, they will want to hire you as a consultant. Now you can see why business consulting is big business in a fast-changing world.

Next, let's talk about why business consulting cannot be a science entirely.

Reference

de Haan, Jac. "Why Do Competitors Open Their Stores Next to One Another?" *YouTube*, uploaded by TED-Ed, 1 October 2012: https://www.youtube.com/watch?v=jILgxeNBK_8&t=53s.

Further Readings

Eaton, B. Curtis, and Richard G. Lipsey. "The Principle of Minimum Differentiation Reconsidered: Some New Developments in the Theory of Spatial Competition." *The Review of Economic Studies*, 17(1), 1975, pp. 27–49.

Hotelling, Harold. "Stability in Competition." *Economic Journal*, 39, March 1929, pp. 41–57.

Similarity: Matters of History and Luck

Prompt Consider flights from Detroit to Las Vegas. Let's say that there is steady and equal demand around the clock. There are three airlines offering flights. Airline X and Airline Y both offer flights at noon. Airline Z offers flights at midnight. The three airlines charge the same price and offer the same services. Are they in equilibrium? What are their market shares? If they are not equal, then tell a story that would explain it. History? Luck?

Keathley: The way I see it, there are two products in this market: flights by airlines X and Y that land in Vegas at 1:30 P.M and flights by airline Z that land at 1:30 A.M. (Flight time from Detroit to Vegas is 4½ hours minus a 3 hour time zone difference). Since the prompt assumes that demand for the flights is uniform around the clock, I am not going to speculate how this demand came about. (Confession: I spent a lot of time speculating only to realize that I did not have to speculate.)

So here we have airlines X and Y offering identical flights at midnight, while airline Z alone offers flights at noon. I would predict that X and Y together have 50% of the market, and Z has the other 50%.

If I had to make up a story about how we got to this point, it would be that airline X and airline Y were in the Detroit-to-Vegas market before Z showed up, each offering only one flight. As to how X and Y ended up clustering at midnight, I can only guess. Perhaps in early days the demand flights was a bit higher at midnight than the rest of the day?

L. W. Lee and A. Keathley, *45 Conversations About Behavioral Economics*, https://doi.org/10.1007/978-3-031-05046-6_11

Fig. 11.1 History and luck in spatial competition

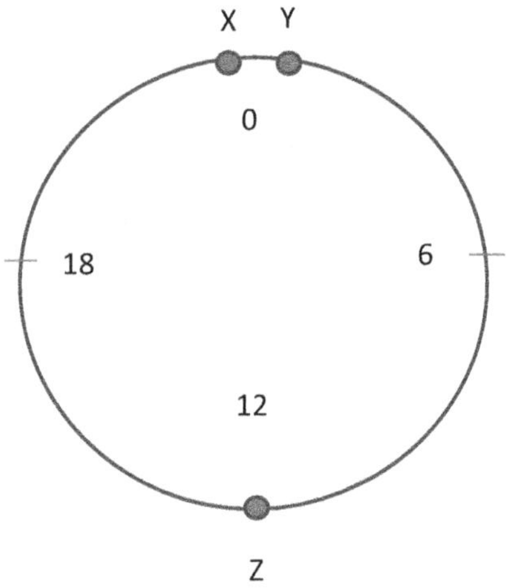

So, as we talked in the earlier prompt, they converged their flights at midnight, with X looking to serve demand from noon to midnight while Y looking to serve demand from midnight to noon. They divided the market 50–50. When the dust had settled on X and Y, airline Z showed up. Z looked around and realized that it could grab 50% of the market by offering flights at noon, which would serve all demand for flights between 6 A.M. and 6 P.M.

Lee: Great story. I am sold. There is just one loose end: Is the new situation a stable equilibrium or not? In other words, do any of the airlines have the incentive to change their flight time when others stay put? If no, then the situation is an equilibrium. If yes, then not an equilibrium.

Keathley: It looks like an equilibrium to me. None of the airline would want to move while the others stay put.

Lee: Right on. In this conversation, I find it easier to work with a clock with 24 hours on it. Figure 11.1 is a picture of the market on such a clock.

Airlines X and Y are paired at midnight, while airline Z sits alone at noon. So, X and Y together have 50% of the market, while Z has the other 50%. Try to move X on the clock and see if it can grab more than 25% of the market? Then, try to move Y and see if it can grab more than 25% of the market. Then try to move Z and see if it can grab more than 50% of the market.

But what explains the fact that Z, the late comer, has double the market share of either of the pioneers, X and Y? Your hunches are fine: only history and luck can explain it. History is X's and Y's destiny. Luck is Z's destiny.

Further Reading

Hotelling, Harold. "Stability in Competition." *Economic Journal*, 39, March 1929, pp. 41–57.

Networks Among Firms: Best Network for Collusion

Prompt Let's say GM, Ford, Toyota, and Honda want to form a network. They want to keep the network as secretive as possible. They ask you to recommend a network structure. Between the cycle network and the star network, which one do you recommend? For each, list the pros and the cons.

Keathley: In this case, I would recommend the cycle network, as in Fig. 12.1.

First and foremost, let's talk about the biggest con to the cycle network: low degree of secrecy. The cycle network at first seems to fall flat on the secrecy measure because every node is connected to 2 other nodes. This leaves a lot of room for conversation among the connected nodes. Connection is great for conversations about business, but not great for secrecy. However, this is less of a problem than at first appears. In this network structure every node is connected to 2 auxiliary nodes, no more and no less. The cycle network excels in fairness: No node is more connected than any other, meaning that no one node has more ability to communicate with the others (or spill the beans on this secret network) than anyone else. The double edge to this is that it takes longer for information to travel through the entire network. Leakage is more likely when information travels through more links.

L. W. Lee and A. Keathley, *45 Conversations About Behavioral Economics*, https://doi.org/10.1007/978-3-031-05046-6_12

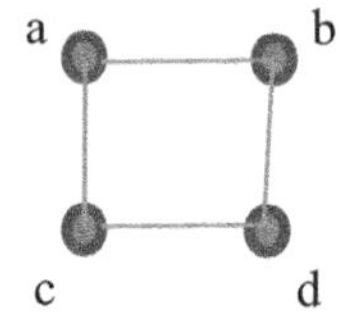

Fig. 12.1 A cycle network

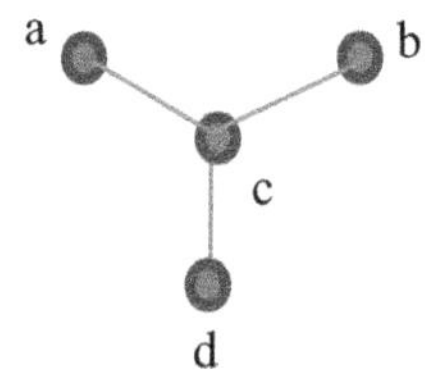

Fig. 12.2 A star network

The star network, as in Fig. 12.2, relies on a central node acting as a directory for the information for the whole network.

The main pro of the star network is its ability to keep the network secretive. But there are cons. This happens because each of the outer nodes can only communicate with the central node. This reduces the communication capabilities of all nodes except the central one. Only the directory node is tasked with moving information around the network, rather than every node taking turns like in the cycle network. The star network minimizes communication but also places large load on the central node. This can clog the network and reduce security if the central node gets sloppy.

All in all, I would recommend the cycle network because it has greater potential for secrecy.

Lee: Network theory is a great tool for telling stories. You have a good, intuitive grasp of it already. Next, build up your toolbox. I would start with two most basic properties of a network:

- the average degree of connection
- the average degree of separation.

The keyword here is "average." So roll up your sleeves and get pencil and paper out. Take the two networks in Figs. 12.1 and 12.2. Do the math and see if you agree with me: The average degree of *connection* equals

2.0 in the cycle network and 1.5 in the star network; the average degree of *separation* equals 1.3 in the cycle network and 1.5 in the star network. These measures support your intuitions earlier: the average member of the cycle network is better connected—and yet more distant from other members—than the average member of the star network.

Your head must be swimming right now. How can we figure out these measures when the network is big, like the human population? Here is hope: Scientists have shown that the average degree of separation among human population on Earth is about 6. That is amazing when we think of the human population as a network with billions of nodes.

Few networks in the real world are complete. The reason is that a network has cost as well as benefit. We talked about transaction cost in a firm before, and that is exactly the nature of cost in a network. (A firm is a network.) As to benefit of network, it comes about in four ways:

- speed of information
- quality of info
- security
- resilience.

There are tradeoffs among these benefits. If you want more of one, you must give up some from the others.

I think the study of network ought to be the first step toward a theory of supply. My colleagues in supply chains will surely agree.

Further Readings

Davletshin, Marat. "7 Ways Network Theory Is Reshaping Supply Chains." *The Sam M. Walton College of Business website*, 25 February 2020: https://walton.uark.edu/insights/network-theory.php.

Goyal, Sanjeev. *Connections: An Introduction to the Economics of Networks*, Princeton University Press, Princeton, NJ, 2007.

CONVERSATION 13

Networks Among Firms: Gary Dinners

Prompt A century ago, US Steel Corporation got into trouble with antitrust laws. An interesting thing that the court considered was "Gary Dinners" among the steel producers. Why did those producers want to have dinners together?

Keathley: According to the paper by Page (2009), "Gary Dinners" were social gatherings and dinners held between 1907 and 1911, and they were hosted by Elbert Henry Gary, the chairman of the board of directors and finance committee of the US Steel Corporation. "Gary Dinners" made it possible for steel producers to get together to discuss how to fix prices. They wanted to fix prices because they felt there was too much "cut-throat" competition in steel prices.

The steel industry has high barriers to entry and startup costs: a steel producer needs to have expertise in the manufacturing process, a large swath of land to put a factory on, and a large amount of money to construct and maintain factory and pay workers. Since so few producers exist, it is relatively simple to get their heads together regularly to fix prices. At dinners, the steel companies can agree to all charge a certain price on a designated product for a specific amount of time. They can also agree on a division of the market among themselves. With the price fixed and the market divided, each producer will make more profit than otherwise.

L. W. Lee and A. Keathley, *45 Conversations About Behavioral Economics*, https://doi.org/10.1007/978-3-031-05046-6_13

Gary Dinners led to the William Taft administration bringing antitrust charges against US Steel, claiming it organized a conspiracy in interstate commerce in violation of the Sherman Anti-Trust Act. This case was taken all the way to the Supreme Court. There the court ruled that "Gary Dinners" did in fact constitute price fixing. However, the court also ruled that US Steel was not a monopoly and did not need to be dissolved because US Steel did not have the market power to manipulate prices.

Lee: The US Steel case is a favorite of mine. Let me share a few tidbits of what I know.

Before Gary Dinners, the steel cartel used to gather at Dirty Mary's Inn, in Upper Michigan. The steel producers wined and dined there. I don't know if they also played golf or not. The inn closed or changed name after the US Steel case. I can't find out what happened to it.

Gary Dinners saved US Steel from breakup. The judge let US Steel off the hook because the judge thought that those dinners were a sign of weakness (competition) rather than a sign of market power. A strong cartel would not have to use dinners to make members feel good about fixing and holding up their prices.

I think the judge here misapplied the antitrust law. The law (specifically, Section 1 of the Sherman Act) does not say that a conspiracy among producers is legal if it is unsuccessful. The law says that any conspiracy is illegal. Here is the first sentence of the law:

> Every contract, combination in the form of trust or otherwise, or conspiracy, in restraint of trade or commerce among the several states, or with foreign nations, is hereby declared to be illegal.

More than 100 years have passed since the US Steel case. Back then, the steel producers apparently thought nothing of antitrust laws. They flouted the laws and got away with them.

What is a takeaway in terms of network theory? The steel cartel back then was more a "complete network" than a star or cycle network. In a complete network, everybody is linked with everybody else; it has the maximum number of links. As we know, links attract attention. You don't want links if you are trying to hide. At least you will try to hide the links by making tacit (rather than explicit) agreement. Examples of tacit agreements are "basing point pricing" and "phase of the moon bidding." The best tacit agreements are the ones we don't know anything about.

US Steel apparently felt that there was no need to hide. And the court agreed.

Reference

Page, William H. "The Gary Dinners and the Meaning of Concerted Action." *SSRN*, 25 February 2009: papers.ssrn.com/sol3/papers.cfm?abstract_id=1349173.

Further Reading

Stelzer, Irwin M. *Selected Antitrust Cases: Landmark Decisions*, 7th edition, Irwin, Homewood, IL, 1986.

Externalities: You Can't Own Air

Prompt When I check local weather on my phone, I often find the Air Quality Index at "Unhealthy for Sensitive Group" or "Poor." It bothers me that I know what is killing me but can't do anything about it. I pay tax on the land on which my house sits. But that does not do a whole lot of good if anyone can pollute the air above my land. Why don't I have property right to the air above my land? What are the problems that must be solved for an effective property-right system for air?

Keathley: The first problem that must be solved for an effective property-rights system for air is the problem of containing air. It is not possible to mark off a portion of air and say: "Dear resident of 12345 Oak Street, this is your air that comes with your land." Since air is mostly gaseous, air will always flow from high pressure areas to low pressure areas. Unless we put every property in a dome, it is not possible to allocate air among us.

The next problem comes with the contents of air. Assuming people have their air bubbles around their land, what happens when your air runs out of oxygen? Do you have to buy more land? Do you have to pay an oxygen tax to get your air oxygenated monthly? In this scenario we are not allowing gas to flow out of your property, so how will you remove the carbon dioxide and carbon monoxide from your bubble? Carbon dioxide and monoxide are made in every house. Also, when you open your bubble

L. W. Lee and A. Keathley, *45 Conversations About Behavioral Economics*, https://doi.org/10.1007/978-3-031-05046-6_14

to leave your property, air moves from high pressure to lower pressure, and you will accidentally "steal" the oxygen from the air on the street.

If a property-right system were established for air in the same way as the property-right system for land, it would be a disaster. Millions of people would asphyxiate while the rich and those born into money will get to breathe clean air. The underlying message to this is that we all collectively own the air and we all must collectively take care of it and protect it.

This is a nightmare. I am beginning to see suffering that I never saw before. What do you do with those who cannot afford to buy air? Air welfare? How do you stop your air from flowing with the wind or mixing about with your neighbor's air? Put all properties in a dome? What happens when your air runs out of oxygen? What if people cannot reoxygenate their domes? What about the air in public places like government buildings, parks, or roads? How do you punish someone who unlawfully consumes your air? How do you catch them? How do you keep your air in your dome when you walk outside? And many, many more problems.

I may have taken this prompt in a different way than it was intended, but I did that to explain why air is a public good in the modern global economy. No one owns the air we breathe because it is impossible to separate air and assign ownership. The unfortunate part is that we all end up polluting the air we breathe.

Lee: Keep up the thinking here. It is scary, but it is great. It has gotten me thinking too about a brave new world. Here is one scenario. One day, I hang out a whole bunch of identical signs around my house:

> All the air above 12345 Oak Street belongs to me. Please note that nobody can breathe or pollute my air without my permission and that violators will be reported to 911. Anyone who wants to buy part of right to my air may call 1-AIR-FOR-SALE.

The next day, neighbor Johnny has a family reunion and he lights up his backyard charcoal grill. All day long, I smell the sugary aroma of burned barbeque sauce. The aroma is pleasant, but it is a pollutant. He must have seen my signs but chosen to ignore them. What do I do? Do I call 911?

We can see why it is difficult to develop property rights about air, surface water, sea level, temperature, ground water, ocean fish that are still wild, and birds that still can fly.

But we need keep thinking in that direction. We already have a few rudimentary tools for building air bubbles, like ventilators, air conditioners, heaters, and air filters. Oh, we have just rediscovered masks, too. Come to think of it, the coronavirus pandemic is the result of the absence of property rights on the air we each breathe. I can't stop the virus from coming into my air space, because I don't have enforceable rights on an air bubble to begin with. Social distancing and masking are ad-hoc parts of a property-rights system for air.

Let's not give up on the idea of privatizing air. A private-property system for air is tough to imagine and build; furthermore, what we should manage to build would be terribly imperfect. But can anything do a worse job than treating air as a "public good"? It has changed the climate on this planet. Air today is a "public bad."

Further Readings

Cowen, Tyler, editor. *Public Goods and Market Failures: A Critical Examination*, Transactions Publishers, New Brunswick, U.S.A, 1992.

Nordhaus, William. *The Climate Casino: Risk, Uncertainty, and Economics for a Warming World*, Yale University Press, New Haven, USA, 2013.

Externalities: The Flint Disaster

Prompt What happened to water in Flint is a tragedy of the commons. Who dumped lead in the river there? Did they have the right to use the river as a common dump?

Keathley: The lead was dumped into the water by all types of local businesses. The Flint River has always been a notoriously polluted river, so polluted that it is reported to have caught fire twice due to the amount of oil in it. These pollutants were dumped by a myriad of industries throughout the years. It started way back in the 1830s. The river was polluted by the lumber industry, followed by the paper mill industry, followed by the carriage industry, and finally by the automobile industry. General Motors, which originated in Flint, appears to be the largest culprit of the pollution. Their factories were constantly flagged for noncompliance with regulations. Nothing ever came about as a result of these companies being flagged except for miniscule fines and fees. Eventually this caught up to them and their factories were destroyed. GM left Flint and moved to another city. However, the damage to Flint River and to Flint residents had already been done. The water was so bad that fish in the water started to asphyxiate from the lack of oxygen. Beyond heavy metals like lead, the river was polluted with ammonia,

L. W. Lee and A. Keathley, *45 Conversations About Behavioral Economics*, https://doi.org/10.1007/978-3-031-05046-6_15

phenol, raw sewage, road salt, industrial fertilizers, and other acidic chemicals. All these together made the water require "10 times the amount of chemicals" to clean compared with other sources of water like Lake Huron.

This came to a head when the drinking water source was switched from the Detroit system to Flint River. All those chemicals in the river corroded the lead pipes and made the water even worse for those that were consuming it. The worst part about it is that it could have been avoided. Dumping is allowed into rivers but there are regulations and EPA guidelines. The amount of pollution in Flint River is the cumulative result of lack of regulation earlier, illegal activity, and failing to punish those illegally dumping into the water. This exemplifies the "tragedy of the commons." If all those who were using the river acted in a responsible way and thought of things other than self-interest, the thousands of people exposed to this water would never have ingested toxic chemicals. Lead is one of the worst compounds a child can ingest during their development and can impair brain function and be fatal.

The tale of the Flint water crisis is one of mismanagement, poor political choices, and greed. When the city was in state management, an active choice was made to cut costs by using Flint River rather than the Detroit water system. Business managers and political leaders together levied this disaster on the city.

Lee: A great report on a tragedy of the commons. We can draw many lessons from it. I think the biggest lesson is: the cure can be worse than the disease. In the Flint case, earlier producers made a mess of the river. They created a disease. So the governor of the State of Michigan slapped regulation on those producers. He sent a guy over to Flint and that was supposed to be the cure. It turned out the cure did not work—the governor's guy did not know what he was doing. The mess became bigger and the disaster followed.

What I am saying is that, when it comes to a public good like river, tragedy is solidly built in. Producers will surely make a mess of the public good. Then we surely send in a regulator to set down rules and policies. Then we surely congratulate ourselves and move on with our own lives. Meanwhile, the regulator makes a bigger mess of the public good because of incompetence, malfeasance, or corruption. We end up with a public bad.

To be fair, perfect regulation is mission impossible. I do not know a perfect regulation by consensus. I bet there will never be one. Meanwhile, I get more and more nervous as I watch how nations are trying to regulate away the biggest market failure of all times: climate change.

Further Readings

Carmody, Tim. "How the Flint River Got so Toxic." *The Verge*, 26 February 2016: https://www.theverge.com/2016/2/26/11117022/flint-michigan-water-crisis-lead-pollution-history.

Carson, Rachel. *Silent Spring*, Houghton Mifflin Company, 1962.

Stern, Nicholas. *Why Are We Waiting? The Logic, Urgency, and Promise of Tackling Climate Change*, The MIT Press, London, England, 2015.

Wagner, Gernot, and Martin L. Weitzman. *Climate Shock: The Economic Consequences of a Hotter Planet*, Princeton University Press, Princeton, NJ, 2015.

PART II

Demand

After hearing our conversations about supply, your head is swimming. How does the average consumer navigate such complex and vast terrain? This is what we will talk about in this part.

Here is a map of our discussion about consumers.

A. Demand by Head
B. Demand by Heart
C. Demand under Peer Pressure
D. Demand under Risk and Uncertainty
E. Demand Nudges
F. Demand Norms
G. Demand Bubbles

(We have 14 conversations about consumers.)

First, we delve into how real-world consumers make decision. We talk about what happens when consumers think with their heads, followed by what happens when they go with their hearts, and then what happens when they form herds. We delve further into the psyche of consumers by discussing how they can be made to do stupid things in places like the friendly local grocery store. We conclude by talking about what terrible things may happen when we simply tell stories back and forth to each other.

By the end of this part, you will have seen someone you vaguely recognize: you yourself. You will have forgiven you yourself for having spent too much money, eaten too much junk food, and chosen a too popular college major.

CHAPTER 16

Demand by Head: Discounting the Future You

Prompt I want to pay you back the money I owe you. There are two options:

(a) $1,000,000 cash now.
(b) $1,200,000 cash five years from now.

Tell me which option you prefer and why.

Keathley:

I would choose to receive the $1,200,000 five years from now. I choose this because of my aversion to investing and my lack of need for a large sum of money now.

To start off, I have a bias against investing. If I received one million dollars now, I would be very skeptical of investing it. Therefore, it would not benefit me to have that money now. I concede the point that a shrewd investor could take the $1,000,000, invest it in bitcoin, and have a higher amount than $1,200,000 five years later. As Richard Thaler (2015) puts it, there are "humans" and there are "econs." Econs are the people that economists imagine when they consider models. They are perfectly rational, and their actions are fully in tune with the laws of supply and demand. However, "econs" do not exist in the real world. Only humans exist in the real world. Humans are people who are willing to drive 30 miles across town to redeem a $1.37 coupon. I am very much a human,

L. W. Lee and A. Keathley, *45 Conversations About Behavioral Economics*, https://doi.org/10.1007/978-3-031-05046-6_16

and I am willing to take a slightly smaller sum of money to avoid the risks of investment.

Incidentally, $1,200,000 in five years would be worth about $1,000,000 today if the average rate of inflation should be 5%. That is a higher average rate than what we have experienced in recent years. So $1,200,000 is likely to turn out to be a better investment anyhow.

This ties into my next reason: I do not think I personally would be able to profit through investment. I believe by simply waiting I will achieve the best possible result. I see the loss aversion bias in me, but regardless I simply rather have guaranteed money than a chance to gain more money through investment.

My last reason for choosing the larger sum of money 5 years down the road is that I simply do not have a need for a large sum of money right now. I hope to attend graduate school down the road, but as of now I am economically stable. I have no student loan debt, I have no housing costs, I have no recurring bills or other outstanding debts. I am sure that I will continue to be economically stable for the next 5 years. Getting a lot of money sooner would tempt me to take school less seriously, make impulse purchases, or give lavish gifts to friends. I feel that if I get the money as a 24 year old man rather than a 21 year old one (I am 20 now), I will use the money to better myself more effectively. This is, again, an argument made out of my heart rather than my head. If I were an "econ," I would take the quicker money. But I am not an econ; I am a human.

Lee: I get it. The human in you takes command in this matter about money; the econ in you has agreed to take a back seat. What is more, the present human you and the future human you have negotiated and come out with the joint statement above.

The statement is perfectly fine. Don't let anyone tell you that you are irrational. The word "irrational" does not exist in the dictionary of behavioral economics.

You may wonder what the econ in you would do if he were to take command in this matter. First of all, the econ you would want to look at me in the eye and ask me to show proof that my offers have been notarized. There must be no risk and uncertainty about money. The other steps can be found in any manual of cost–benefit analysis (CBA).

Let me dwell on CBA a little, given that it is still the gospel in business and public policy circles. You—the econ you—would have to pick discount rates and use them to find the present discounted value (PDV). I say discount "rates" because $1,200,000 is five years out, so the econ would have to discount it continuously over the five-year period using discount rate that may very well vary over this period of time. Since no one can predict this time function, the econ you will have to assume it. Here the econ you will get an earful of instructions if he asks for expert advice.

I don't have expert advice on discount rate for the econ you. I will mention the nominal interest rate on 5-year US government bonds. If it is 1.0%, then use 1.01 as the annual total discount rate. I am not going to elaborate the math here, because the ground beneath it is terribly shaky. The bottom line is that there is no such thing as the "right" or "optimal" rate of discount in CBA.

In the final analysis, discounting over time is an ethics problem, not a finance problem. It involves bargaining among many yous: econ and human, present and future, etc. Moral philosophers know best how "multiple selves" work things out, or not.

By the way, consider the same problem with much smaller amounts of money. Say, the options are; $10 today versus $12 five years from now. I bet that now you will want the $10 today. That means the present-day you wins and the future you loses.

Reference

Thaler, Richard H. *Misbehaving: The Making of Behavioral Economics*, W. W. Norton, New York, NY, 2015.

Further Readings

Herron, Janna. "Winning the Lottery: Should You Take the Annual Payments or Lump Sum?" *USA Today*, 12 February 2020: https://www.usatoday.com/story/money/2020/02/12/winning-lottery-take-lump-sum-annual-payments/4736439002/.

Schelling, Thomas C. *Choice and Consequence*, Harvard University Press, Cambridge, MA, 1984.

CONVERSATION 17

Demand by Head: To Marry or Not to Marry

Prompt You are considering marriage. You want to make the decision scientifically. So, you are doing a "cost–benefit analysis." Make sure you recognize that the costs and the benefits are mostly in the future. Show how and what you decide.

Keathley: Immediate Costs: monetary costs of a marriage license, monetary costs of a wedding/honeymoon, opportunity cost of not being able to spend the time I spend on planning the wedding doing other things like working or leisure activities, opportunity cost of the time and money spent on my fiancé, loss of opportunity to marry another partner.

Future Costs: opportunity cost of the time and money spent with my spouse, opportunity cost of being faithful to my spouse rather than looking for a better partner, higher cost of living (paying for some of my wife's things), monetary and opportunity cost of buying gifts, possibility of emotional instability (arguing, cheating, death of a spouse, infertility), and possibility of financial ruin via divorce.

Immediate Benefits: Emotional wellbeing (love/gratification/less worry about the future), gifts from wedding attendees, spouse's current assets.

Future Benefits: Emotional wellbeing (love/gratification/less worry about the future), second household income, spouse's future assets, companionship, lower taxes.

L. W. Lee and A. Keathley, *45 Conversations About Behavioral Economics*, https://doi.org/10.1007/978-3-031-05046-6_17

Taking into consideration all these costs and benefits, I believe that I would go through with marrying the person. Financially, marriage may be a poor choice if I am or will be much richer than my partner. But I am not an econ; I am a human. Especially as a young human with many years of working and hopefully financial prosperity ahead of me, I value emotional gain much higher than financial gain. I am willing to take on the risks now because in the event that I do end up in financial or emotional ruin because of this marriage, I have a lot of time to try and make up for my losses. The only resource that I do not have the ability to regain is time.

Lee: Wow, these are a lot of pros and cons. If you are going to be a true hardhead about marriage, you need to take three more steps. First, you need to get on the internet and study those cost–benefit charts and tables for marriage (Moran 2021; Livingston 2015). Make sure you do not miss any cost and benefit. Second, you need to assign values to costs and benefits. For future costs and future benefits, you need to find present discounted values (PDVs). Third, find the total PDV of costs and subtract it from the total PDV of benefits. If the net is positive, get married with that person. If negative, forget it—or find someone else and redo the numbers. Oh, I forgot another thing here: you will need to ask your partner if she is an econ or a human, and what she thinks.

Now you may ask: how many humans do cost–benefit analysis of marriage like that? I don't know, but I know that Charles Darwin tried (Popova 2012). I do notice that both Darwin and you left out something in the analysis: children. Neither of you mentioned children as a cost or benefit. I don't know about you, but Darwin had 10 children with his wife. Apparently he counted children as a big benefit in his revised cost–benefit analyses of marriage.

What are two takeaways here? First, marriage is an extremely complex problem. Second, when faced with a complex problem, we can solve it by doing what our emotions and gut feelings tell us to do. In behavioral economics, emotions and gut feelings are called "fast-and-frugal heuristics." Gerd Gigerenzer (2014) writes a lot on this topic. His favorite example of a fast-and-frugal heuristic is "the gaze heuristic." Say, you want to catch a flying baseball. You don't sit down and try to solve a bunch of dynamic equations of motion. You simply run toward it, keeping your gaze on the ball. It's not that hard. Humans do it. Animals like dogs and eagles excel at it.

Getting married is like catching a baseball. Trust it to your emotions and gut feelings. We all know the heuristic that humans and animals (but not econs) use for catching the right partner: "love."

References

Gigerenzer, Gerd. *Risk Savvy: How to Make Good Decisions*, Viking, New York, 2014.

Livingston, Amy. "Financial Benefits of Marriage vs. Being Single—What's Better?" Money *Crashers*, 24 November 2015: https://www.moneycrashers.com/financial-benefits-marriage-single/.

Moran, Porcshe. "The Economics of a Successful Marriage." *Investopedia*, 17 June 2021: https://www.investopedia.com/financial-edge/0411/apply-economics-for-a-successful-marriage.aspx.

Popova, Maria. "Charles Darwin's List of the Pros and Cons of Marriage." *Brainpickings*, 2012, accessed on 4 September 2021: https://www.brainpickings.org/2012/08/14/darwin-list-pros-and-cons-of-marriage/.

Further Readings

Gigerenzer, Gerd. *Risk Savvy: How to Make Good Decisions*, Viking, New York, 2014.

Gladwell, Malcolm. *Blink: The Power of Thinking Without Thinking*, Back Bay Books, New York, NY, 2007.

CONVERSATION 18

Demand by Heart: Gambling

Prompt For $5, you may play one of two gambles:

(a) fair coin flip: If head, you get $10; if tail, you get nothing.
(b) super lotto: You get to choose one out of 10 million numbers. By random drawing, if the number that turns up is your number, you get $50 million; if it is not your number, you get nothing.

Which gamble appeals to you more? How do you make that decision?

Keathley: The fair coin flip game appeals more to me. Most obviously because the odds are so much better. (I don't care that much about expected values, which are $5 in both gambles.) Beyond just odds, the opportunity to win life changing money will not comfort me when I have lost my $5 dollars and must wake up and get back to whatever I was doing. If I won the $5, it may not change my life, but it would make me happy for the day. The small gain is better to my brain than the loss that I would face in the super lotto.

Beyond the statistics, it just feels better to win a little something rather than losing by taking a chance on something that is not realistically going to happen. Everyone dreams of winning the lottery and what extravagant things they would spend their winnings on. However, most people realize that it will likely never happen. There is a chance, but it is such a small one that it is effectively zero. Everyone also hates losing. Some people like

L. W. Lee and A. Keathley, *45 Conversations About Behavioral Economics*, https://doi.org/10.1007/978-3-031-05046-6_18

me value preventing a small loss more than getting a shot at a big gain. This is a classic case of loss aversion. My first instinct was to take the first gamble because it will feel much better to win an extra $5 so I walk away with $10 at the end of the day, than to lose the $5 in my hand now and walk away with nothing at the end of the day. If I walk away with $10, I go and get lunch, and it makes me feel lucky and happy for the rest of my day. If I walk away with $0, I lament my awful lotto-picking skills and feel bad that I threw $5 away at an essentially unwinnable game.

Lee: Good show. It is a confession of a human gambler. I appreciate how emotions play in your decision.

Let me tell you how I choose between the two gambles: If I am home alone paying utility bills and credit card debts, my mood will be somber. I will choose A, the fair coin flip. But if I am with friends playing slot machines at a Las Vegas casino—and having free drinks—I will definitely choose B, the super lotto.

So, "context" matters a lot to me. Does context determine which part of the brain goes to work? Absolutely! We use different parts of our brain in different contexts (Kahneman 2011). This is something that people in marketing know best. They use advertising to create the "right context" (in other words, the "right mood") for consumers to buy that pair of jeans, or that car, or that lotto.

Keathley: What is it about being in a casino that would make you choose the riskier option? Besides alcohol and the obvious loud, shiny slot machines, what else about casinos that make us more willing to part with our hard earned cash? The design of casinos can tell a lot about this. Casinos are bright and vibrant but have no windows. This causes people to lose track of time and stay way longer, which causes the house to win more. Also, the places where you trade your chips and tickets for cash is usually in the very back, meaning that you have to walk past all the glistening games and tables to collect your winnings. Beyond the layout and design of casinos what else do they do to influence your decision making? Casinos move dealers from table to table more often when a gambler is winning big. They hope it will cause him/her to feel unlucky, thus betting more conservatively, or getting him/her to stop all together. Casinos know how to create contexts so as to nudge customers.

Lee: You know a lot about casinos. What's going on?

In any case, "context"—or "frame"—is a most fascinating thing. Whenever I talk about frame, I think of the Müller-Lyer picture in Fig. 18.1.

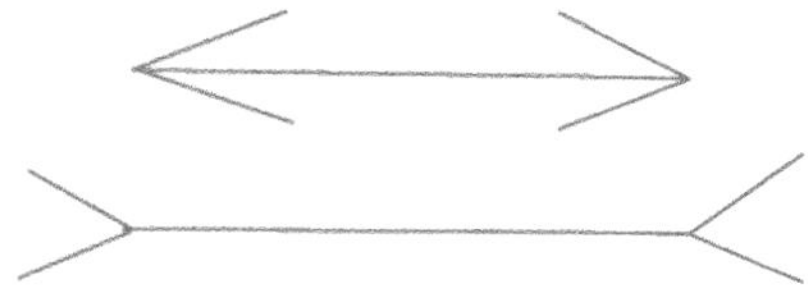

Fig. 18.1 Which line is longer?

Which line is longer? You can tell by looking at them or measuring them. Warning: You will come out with different answers. That is what illusion is all about.

Reference

Kahneman, Daniel. *Thinking Fast and Slow*, Farrar, Strauss and Giroux, New York, NY, 2011.

Further Reading

Duke, Annie. *How to Decide: Simple Tools for Making Better Choices*, Portfolio, Penguin Publishing Group, 2020.

Demand by Heart: The Marshmallow Test

Prompt The Marshmallows Test is designed to see if a person (or animal) prefers gratification now to gratification later. It goes something like: "You may choose between 5 marshmallows now and 7 marshmallows an hour later." You pass the test if you choose to have more later. Krugman (2020) says that Americans are failing the Marshmallow Test during Covid-19. What's he saying?

Keathley: In America's "Marshmallow Test," there is the option to reopen states now and live life as if the virus did not exist, and there is also the option to be disciplined, hunkering down with strict social distancing, mask wearing, and social safety net programs. Between the two options, there is a tradeoff. The longer we as a society go locked down, the better life will be when we reopen. For example, if the U.S. opened up every state completely today, society would reap the least reward as cases and deaths soar. On the other hand, if the whole country strapped in and followed all the Covid protocols and measures for two months, we would see fewer cases and deaths when we reopen. If America as a whole could hunker down for four months, there would be even fewer cases and deaths after reopening. So on and so forth. The tradeoff between freedom today and freedom in the future is at the core of this choice.

Krugman sees Americans as mostly leaning toward having the marshmallows now. We are choosing what will benefit us today rather than what will benefit us in the future. What is even more unfortunate is that

L. W. Lee and A. Keathley, *45 Conversations About Behavioral Economics*, https://doi.org/10.1007/978-3-031-05046-6_19

those who are choosing to follow all guidelines now will still likely live in a future environment that has massive cases and deaths. This is another example of the "tragedy of the commons." Since a large portion of the population is not choosing masks, masks will become less effective in the future for those that wear them now.

By the way, I can think of a stronger version of the Marshmallow Test. Imagine that marshmallow is a plant that produces seeds that can be planted easily to grow more marshmallows. Suppose that America has only one marshmallow. Rather than taking the one marshmallow we have and planting it, a lot of people in the U.S. are happily chowing down that one-and-only-one marshmallow with no regard for the future. This pandemic has really highlighted the shortsightedness of the US population.

Lee: Good marshmallow stories. I second your opinion that the virus pandemic is a penalty for our failing the Marshmallow Test.

Our failure at the test shows that we don't make decisions like the "rational consumer." This consumer is a computer program that manages a single, well-defined performance function. I am not that computer program. I work with impatience, shortsightedness, regret, you name it. These are stuff in my warm, racing heart. They don't belong in my cool, steadfast head.

We can see better what is going on in a heart if we think of a person as the domicile of multiple selves, rather than a single self. (Adam Smith—yes, that Adam Smith—thought so when he introduced the "impartial spectator" in *The Theory of Moral Sentiments*.) Do you not sometime feel as if there are several yous living in one body, cooperating and conflicting in turn? Do you not sometimes hear conversation between the several yous? What about the angel and devil versions of yourself? Or when you are torn between stopping to help someone in need and continuing to walk to that meeting you are late to? Fig. 19.1 shows that the two of you are negotiating something.

Once we get out of the straightjacket of the single-minded rational consumer, we can understand ourselves a lot better. Take addiction to alcohol, for example. We drink, regret and quit, just to drink again, regret again and quit again... This cycle of drinking and quitting is exhausting. Psychologists view it as a struggle between two selves alternating in command. Economists view it as the result of pure madness. That is why addicts get help from psychologists, not economists.

Fig. 19.1 The two-self you

By the way, cuttlefish do fine on the Marshmallow Test (Saplakoglu 2021). That is something to chew on.

References

Krugman, Paul. "America Fails the Marshmallow Test." *The New York Times*, 9 June 2020: https://www.nytimes.com/2020/06/09/opinion/coronavirus-reopening-marshmallow-test.html?action=click&module=Opinion&pgtype=Homepage.

Saplakoglu, Yasemin. "Cuttlefish Show Self-Control, Pass 'Marshmallow Test'." *Live Science*, 3 March 2021: https://www.livescience.com/cuttlefish-pass-marshmallow-test.html.

Further Readings

Kingwell, Mark. "Want to Make Better Public-Health Citizens? Give People What Feels Good Now." *MACLEA'S*, 20 August 2020: https://www.macleans.ca/opinion/want-to-make-better-public-health-citizens-give-people-what-feels-good-now/.

Simon, Herbert A. *Models of Bounded Rationality, Behavioral Economics, and Business Organizations*, volume 2, MIT Press, Cambridge, 1982.

Smith, Adam. *The Theory of Moral Sentiments*, Liberty Classics edition, Indianapolis, Indiana, 1759/1976.

CONVERSATION 20

Demand Under Peer Pressure: Picking Your Shoes

Prompt Do you remember the last time when you bought a pair of shoes? Would you say that you considered only comfort and price? Or did you worry about how other people think when they see you in those shoes? How did you learn about those shoes?

Keathley: I just recently bought a pair of shoes for myself and for my girlfriend. It was our anniversary, and she mentioned that she would like this specific pair of grey slip-on shoes from the Vans Company. I have 12+ pairs of shoes from this company, so I was well aware of the quality of these shoes. This meant that I was happy to oblige and give Vans my business. Since I already know the quality of this firm's shoes, I considered price heavily. She told me about these shoes in early July, and our anniversary was not until the middle of September. I had time on my side and I was determined to wait until a sale occurred to pull the trigger and make the purchase. A bargain was much more important than when this box shows up on my doorstep, because no matter what day the shoes come, she would not be trying them on until September 18th. If a sale did not occur by then, I would still make the purchase regardless. A sale did occur, and I was happy about that.

When buying my own shoes, I considered price even more heavily. I made sure to try and pick a pair that got me as close to the $100 total price point that would entitle me to $25 off my order. As with her shoes, the comfort was assumed so I looked solely at shoes that fit the price

L. W. Lee and A. Keathley, *45 Conversations About Behavioral Economics*, https://doi.org/10.1007/978-3-031-05046-6_20

criteria and I would enjoy wearing. I did not consider what others would think of my shoes because at the end of the day, my mantra is that as long as I believe that I look good, that is all that matters. I finally settled on a pair of off-white shoes that I was shown in an advertisement sent to my email. It seems that no matter how many times that I unsubscribe from their mailing list, they will continue to send me advertisements for their latest and greatest shoes. Their efforts are often rewarded, as despite my annoyance about how often they send such advertisement, I continually open their messages and now I have even made a purchase because of it.

Now I realize that the contexts of those decisions were different. If I had been browsing randomly rather than shopping for a gift, I might have been more influenced by other factors. As someone who has many pairs of shoes, I am in no danger of not having a pair of shoes to wear on a daily basis. I only shop for new Vans out of excess. As a result, when I browse their website, I need a very strong nudge (maybe a "push") to make me fork over the cash rather than simply daydream about my hypothetical ownership.

Lee: For the longest time, I have been thinking about how we as consumers make decisions. How do we make decisions when we buy shoes, groceries, alcohol, stocks, houses, cars, and all of the other stuff? I have come to the conclusion that, as consumers, we very much depend on each other for making decisions. For example, we frequently drink with friends and business associates. Why? When people ingest alcohol, they exhibit less inhibition. After a couple of beers, I begin to talk more and talk about things I otherwise would not. Meanwhile, others are getting boozy and beginning to babble about things that they otherwise would not. For better or for worse, we gather new information about each other during the conversation. After the party, our opinions about Vans shoes and that business deal will be different than before the party.

A great tool for thinking about consumer decisions is network theory. Figure 20.1 shows consumers shopping for shoes. Most belong to networks, large and small. Some are very well connected. Two are loners.

We call network effects on our demand behavior by different names: peer pressure, conformism, herding, bandwagon effect, club goods, etc.

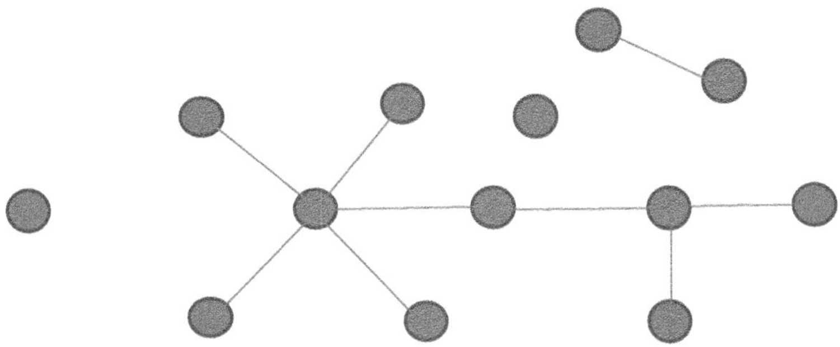

Fig. 20.1 A demand network

Further Readings

Gladwell, Malcolm. *The Tipping Point: How Little Things Can Make a Big Difference*, Little, Brown and Company, New York, 2006.

Kadushin, Charles. *Understanding Social Networks: Theories, Concepts, and Findings*, Oxford University Press, New York, NY, 2012.

Tsipursky, Gleb. "Beware of Your Friends' Influence on Your Shopping Decisions." *Psychology Today*, 16 November 2020: https://www.psychologytoday.com/us/blog/intentional-insights/202011/beware-your-friends-influence-your-shopping-decisions.

Demand Under Peer Pressure: Your Last Hangover

Prompt Do you remember the last time when you had a little too much to drink? Was it social drinking? What was the nature of advertising of the beverage?

Keathley: The last time when I had too much to drink was at a goodbye party for a friend of mine during the summer. I would describe it as social drinking for most of the night. There were a decent number of people there. We played drinking games. There were times when the group went outside to get food, walked around, or did other things that drunken people do, and I often stayed behind. Staying behind did not cause me to feel like I should stop drinking. I certainly was not playing drinking games by myself, but I was casually sipping my drink and watching the TV. Overall, it should be categorized as social drinking because if I had been alone or in a smaller group of people I would have drunk significantly less and maybe not at all.

The beverage that I was enjoying was Jameson Irish Whiskey and ginger ale. This cocktail itself is obviously not advertised, but its components definitely are. The actual alcohol, Jameson, is one of the largest whiskey brands sold in the U.S., and it is advertised relatively often. Off the top of my head, I can remember seeing their "Join in with Jameson" TV commercial quite vividly. This commercial shows various groups of young, healthy adults laughing, dancing, playing pool, going from bar to bar, and generally having a good time. This is very reminiscent of the beer

L. W. Lee and A. Keathley, *45 Conversations About Behavioral Economics*, https://doi.org/10.1007/978-3-031-05046-6_21

commercials that you talked about in class. An alcoholic drink, which by no stretch of the imagination is healthy, is marketed in a way that shows healthy people having fun. This gets people to associate the beverage with health, friendship, youth, and fun. The Canada Dry Ginger Ale is advertised in a much different way from the whiskey and from other sodas. I could not think of an ad off the top of my head for Canada Dry, so I looked up a recent one. It plays very much into the Asian heritage of ginger root and other soft stereotyping. The ad revolves around a man sitting in an artificial pond and waterfall calmly talking about the real ginger in his pop and its calming effects. The ad plays very much into calmness and the serenity and tranquility of ginger root. The ad ends with the man being yelled at after it is revealed that he is sitting in a shopping mall display. The guard is offered the soda, lowers his tone, and joins the man in the pond.

These ads are designed to trigger the buy impulse for these beverages. The alcohol ad downplays the negative health aspects and highlights the fun of partying on beach and at bar. The soda ad tries to appeal to young adults looking to unwind, destress, or otherwise just be calm. I think that the alcohol ad is much more effective. I don't know anyone who believes that a tiny amount of ginger extract makes a sugary pop healthy, while I know lots of people who associate alcohol with fun and youthful exuberance.

Lee: An interesting story told with deep insight! Your story reminds me of my youthful days when I drank beer. Not just socially, but also solitarily. I started to feel not so good. I would often ask myself: Why am I drinking so much?

One day, I decided to find an answer. That was the beginning of a most interesting research project, funded by National Institute of Alcohol and Alcohol Abuse. The first thing I noticed was that I drank a lot more at parties than at home alone—well, not quite alone, as my dog T-Bone always sat with me. As I searched for literature on that "social drinking" behavior, I found a lot of it. The catch word is "drinking context." Alcohol ads rarely show an old man sitting in a large sofa holding a bottle of vodka. Rather, they show groups of friends and relatives toasting each other on a deck during sunset. I paid particular attention to TV beer commercials, and I found that they never talk about what is in the beer. But for the picture of a beer bottle at the corner of the TV screen, they are all about young, healthy, beautiful people laughing and playing volleyball on a beach just before sunset (Lee 1997). I don't watch TV commercials anymore, but what you are telling me is that little has changed.

Keathley: Traditional economics would say that advertisements like the beach volleyball commercial should have no impact on a rational consumer. However, we know that people are very much impacted by advertisements, peer pressure, and public perception of a product. Growing up I would never have been caught dead in a "Champion" brand shirt or pair of shoes. However, today, this is a very popular brand of clothing for young people. Hip-hop artists and other celebrities with a large cultural presence among young people started wearing "Champion" clothes ironically and eventually they started wearing them unironically and today I see people wearing them all the time. This undoubtedly would not be the case without these celebrities making it "cool" to wear these clothes.

Reference

Lee, Li Way. "Persuasive Advertising and Socialization." *International Journal of the Economics of Business*, 4(2), 1997, pp. 203–214.

Further Reading

Joormann, Jutta. "Why Adolescents Make Riskier Choices When With Their Peers." *Psychology Today*, 31 January 2020: https://www.psychologytoday.com/us/blog/thoughts-and-feelings/202001/why-adolescents-make-riskier-choices-when-their-peers.

Demand Under Risk and Uncertainty: Insurance on Your Dream Car

Prompt You are buying your dream car. You want to consider collision insurance. The insurance agent offers the following information:

(i) The average risk of collision: 1% in 12 months
(ii) The average cost of car repair: $10,000
(iii) Collision insurance premium: $200 for 12 months with no deductible
(iv) Most owners of new cars buy collision insurance.

Do you buy the collision insurance or not? Tell me how you make that decision.

Keathley: My dream car is a Ford 1970 Mach 1 Mustang in Grabber Green paint, customized with an electric motor and automatic transmission. A perfectly restored stock edition of one of these cars will set you back around $80,000 with another $100,000 likely tied up in converting it from a gas engine with a manual transmission to an electric motor and automatic transmission. Needless to say, this would be a large investment. If I were in the position to purchase a vehicle like this, I would have to be rather wealthy and well off. In that case, cost would be the least of my concerns when it comes to purchasing a "bucket list" car. Then I would probably purchase the collision insurance for no reason other than simplicity in decision making.

L. W. Lee and A. Keathley, *45 Conversations About Behavioral Economics*, https://doi.org/10.1007/978-3-031-05046-6_22

My first thought was the sunk cost fallacy. In this situation, I already have a lot of money sunk into this car and no fault insurance. What does a thousand dollars of collision insurance per year matter when I have already paid so much money? This is obviously a heuristic in reasoning.

The other thing that would lead me to buying the collision insurance is the endowment effect. Perhaps not in the traditional sense of this heuristic, but I think it still applies here. The endowment effect states that I value my item more after I have owned it. It is worth more to me once it is in my endowment. It is like purchasing a shirt for \$30 one minute and then not willing to give it up for \$40. In my case, I would value this car so much that I would never sell it. I would buy anything that could keep it in my possession. So, I would buy the collision insurance on my Mustang.

As for the cold-blooded math, it still supports my decision to buy collision. The annual expected cost of repair is the average cost of repair (\$10,000) multiplied by the annual risk of collision (1%). So the expected value of the annual collision policy is

$$\$10,000 \times 0.01 = \$100$$

This is less than the annual cost of the collision policy at \$200. At first sight, then, the collision policy appears to be a bad deal. But my Mustang is not the average car; a collision repair job will cost \$50,000 upwards. So the value of the insurance policy is at least

$$\$50,000 \times 0.01 = \$500$$

This is more than the annual cost of the collision policy at \$200.

Do I make any sense here?

Lee: Yes, you make a lot of sense. The last bit of "cold-blooded math" is standard fare of risk analysis. Risk, however, is not the whole story about insurance. As your story shows, there are other things involved in the decision. Let me talk about a couple of them: uncertainty and the endowment effect.

Figure 22.1 is a shot at describing uncertainty. The climber sees one side of the mountain and knows the risk of falling on that side. But the climber cannot see the other side of the mountain (and does not have a drone to help see). That means the climber faces uncertainty on the other side. Risk is about "known unknowns," while uncertainty is about "unknown unknowns."

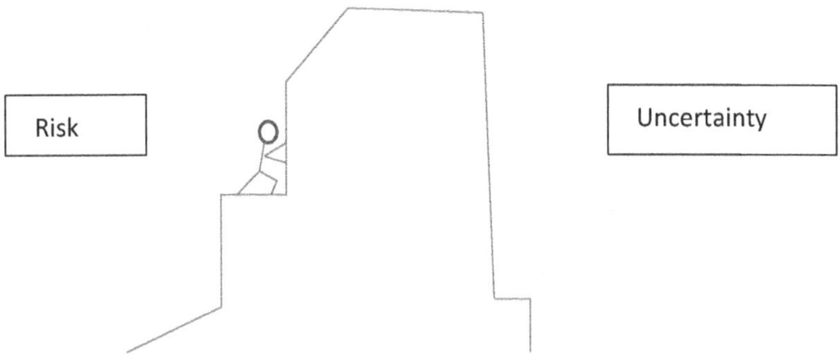

Fig. 22.1 Risk and uncertainty

In the case of your car, the risk of collision is known, but the risks of theft and falling into potholes are unknown. So you face both risk and uncertainty.

About the endowment effect, let me share with you a true story. In early summer of 1976, I needed a car to move from New York City to my first job in Pennsylvania. (I had never driven a car before.) I asked my good neighbor Jim for help with finding me a car. His eyes just lit up. He said that the lady four doors down the street had a car in her garage. She had retired and rarely drove anymore. Few people knew she had a car. However, Jim had seen it, and he told me that it was a beauty. Jim encouraged me to go and knock on her door. He offered to go with me.

She was happy to show us her car. It was a true beauty: a two-door 1964 Dodge Dart, light cream, with barely twenty thousand miles on it. I immediately fell in love, I promised her that I would take good care of her car, and I would give her what she asked for it: $1000. (Don't laugh; those were 1976 dollars.) Long story short, she took my offer under the condition that I leave the car in her garage until I have learned how to drive and gotten the driver's license. The next day, the phone rang. It was her. She murmured a few words and started to cry. I figured out that she did not want to sell me the car anymore. I told her I wanted to see her in person about this. I found Jim and the two of us went over to her. After Jim and I repeated our promise to take good care of her car, we sat there quietly.... I don't remember for how long. I still remember her tears. In the end, she relented.

In her case, the endowment effect was not about money. She did not bring up the matter of money. All she wanted was my reassurance that I would take good care of her car.

Further Readings

Thaler, Richard H. *Misbehaving: The Making of Behavioral Economics*, W. W. Norton, New York, NY, 2015.

The Decision Lab. "Why Do We Value Items More If They Belong to Us?" accessed on 25 August 2021: https://thedecisionlab.com/biases/endowment-effect/.

Demand Under Risk and Uncertainty: A Fast and Frugal Way to Make Money

Prompt We don't know much about all those stocks and bonds out there. We know they have risks, but we don't know their risks in terms of probabilities of good, bad, and ugly outcomes. So what we face is uncertainty. How do we make decisions about investment in the face of uncertainty? Gerd Gigerenzer recommends the "I/N heuristic." What is that? How does it differ from the "index heuristic"?

Keathley: The "1/N" is a heuristic for investing. It means that the investor divides the money equally among several recognized options. If the investor had $1,000,000 to invest and were considering 5 firms, then the investor would buy $200,000 of each firm. For this prompt, I read a post by Noren (2010). Here is what I learned.

Gigerenzer says that Harry Markowitz chose to invest his money by means of the 1/N heuristic. Markowitz was the winner of the 1990 Nobel Prize in Economics, for his work on "modern portfolio theory." Gigerenzer (2014) cited the conclusion of a study comparing asset allocation theories: "There is no single model that consistently delivers a Sharpe ratio or a CEO return that is higher than that of the 1/N portfolio, which also has a very low turnover." I do not understand these theories, but I do understand that the fast-and-frugal 1/N heuristic can be as effective as any of the fancy strategies.

The 1/N heuristic is very reminiscent of herd mentality and of the recognition heuristic. They share the principle that people tend to go

L. W. Lee and A. Keathley, *45 Conversations About Behavioral Economics*, https://doi.org/10.1007/978-3-031-05046-6_23

with what everyone else is doing. If most people are choosing to invest in firms A, B, and C, then I am likely to do fine by following them into A, B, and C.

Like the index heuristic, the 1/N heuristic uses recognition as a factor in making choice. (A stock index like NASDAQ is well recognized.) Unlike the index heuristic, the 1/N heuristic allocates investment equally in the beginning. (NASDAQ does not allocate money equally among firms in its portfolio.)

Heuristics like 1/N work where there is indeed wisdom in a crowd. Imagine a group of 20 students discussing their math homework. You are sitting there listening to them. They get the first 5 answers right, but when they come to question number 6, they say a different answer than you have. Even if you are confident in your answer you may feel pressured to change your answer. At that time you notice that the smartest kid in the class is leading the discussion. You may think to yourself: They have been right the last 5 times and Rebecca is the valedictorian....

Oh, I read in Altman (2012) an experiment on the name recognition heuristic. Which city has the greater population: San Antonio or San Diego? They ask the question to Germans and Americans. Americans are familiar with both cities but only 62% get it right. Germans have only heard of San Diego so 100% choose it and get it correct. Fun fact: this is no longer true. San Antonio has overtaken San Diego in population!

Lee: While listening to you about fast-and-frugal heuristics, I thought of another example in Gigerenzer (2014): medical diagnosis. We know that physicians today use all kinds of diagnostic equipment to try to figure out the "right" treatment. However, there is one area of medicine where the use of diagnostic equipment can be dangerous: emergency medicine. Physicians in emergency room must make split-second decisions about what is wrong and what needs to be done right away to save a life. If the patient has stopped breathing, the physician immediately hooks the patient to a ventilator. The physician does not sit down and go through the diagnostic chart for "Shortness of Breath" first. So, emergency room doctors are similar to baseball players: Their skills are based on their instincts rather than detailed calculations. I think this example is pretty cool.

Keathley: Now I am thinking about what people do in extreme driving scenarios. When people are trying to avoid an accident, they do not consider whether their maneuvers are legal or recommended by driving school. Instead, the "thinking fast" part of their brains takes over. Our fast thinking is able to make us to do things that we would not have considered even if we had the time to sit down and weigh the options.

Lee: Great example. Avoiding a car accident is a complex problem, indeed. Gigerenzer figures that the more complex is the problem, the simpler is the solution. He calls it "less-is-more heuristic." Gladwell (2007) calls it "blink."

Back to making money, I think of John Bogle. He was the founder of investment company Vanguard. Listen to his lament about how most humans invest: "We ignore the real diamonds of simplicity, seeking instead the illusory rhinestones of complexity" (Bogle, 2009, p. 23). If you know anything about Vanguard, you cannot but conclude that he is right.

References

Altman, Morris. *Behavioral Economics for Dummies*, John Wiley and Sons Canada, Ltd., 2012.

Bogle, John C. *Enough: True Measures of Money, Business, and Life*, Wiley, Hoboken, NJ, 2009.

Gigerenzer, Gerd. *Risk Savvy: How to Make Good Decisions*, Viking, New York, NY, 2014.

Gladwell, Malcolm. *Blink: The Power of Thinking Without Thinking*, Back Bay Books, New York, NY, 2007.

Noren, Anders. "Heuristics and Robustness in Asset Allocation: The 1/N Rule, 'Hard' Constraints and Fractional Kelly Strategies." *Macroresilience*, 8 July 2010: www.macroresilience.com/2010/07/08/heuristics-and-robustness-in-asset-allocation/.

Further Readings

Bogle, John C. *Enough: True Measures of Money, Business, and Life*, Wiley, Hoboken, NJ, 2009.

Gigerenzer, Gerd. *Rationality for Mortals: How People Cope with Uncertainty*, Oxford University Press, New York, NY, 2008.

Demand Nudges: Nudges in Supermarket

Prompt A supermarket is a "choice architecture." Nudges are everywhere: labels, music, shelf arrangements, layout, promotions, lighting, free samples.... Next time you go to your favorite supermarket, find 5 nudges that you never noticed before.

Keathley: I went to the local Meijer in search of groceries and nudges. Most of the ones that I noticed I had heard of before, but never before had I considered how powerful they are, even after I know they are there. The first one that I noticed was that the most expensive products in an isle are at eye level. For example, if I want to buy the Meijer brand corn flakes, I have to look at either the bottom or top shelf. The most expensive and name brand are going to be at eye level. This is a good nudge because if I was shopping quickly I would instantly grab the product at eye level, thus spending more money. There is one major exception: cereal. A lot of the time the name brands—incredibly unhealthy cereals—are on a lower level. The store does this because the lower level is at the perfect height for children to grab that super sugary cereal.

The next nudge that I noticed was that the store was always playing relaxing music. This music made me not want to rush around the store. Staying longer almost always equals spending more. The third thing that I noticed was the store layout. Much like a casino that hides the money exchange in the back, this store makes sure to put popular products very far away from each other. I had to walk from one side of the store to the

L. W. Lee and A. Keathley, *45 Conversations About Behavioral Economics*, https://doi.org/10.1007/978-3-031-05046-6_24

other to get the next item on my list. I ended up picking up stuff not on my list.

Fourth, I noticed that baskets are absolutely massive. A shopping cart when I was younger was not able to contain all the groceries. We used to have to use 2 or 3 carts. Now, we usually barely fill one. When a basket is larger, we get the urge (nudge?) to measure up to it by filling it up. Anything that keeps consumers in the store longer is guaranteed to make them buy more items and therefore increase the store's revenue.

The last thing that I noticed was how the checkout area is set up. The checkout area has lots of candies and mints. These are quick impulse buys that parents often make to force their small children to quit whining. The checkout lane is the last place in the store where the shopper will be able to buy something. Besides, shoppers are usually rushing to get out of the store. All the other nudges have caused shoppers to stay in the store longer than planned, and they are off their schedule for the day by the time they reach the checkout area. So, when people get to the register, they are frazzled and very susceptible to impulse purchases. The $4 candy bar seems like a quick and tasty reward that you deserve for buying groceries. However, 20 minutes later many of us go "how did I spend that much money on a tiny candy bar!" The store has achieved its goal. Similar items they stock at the register prey on shoppers' strong emotions.

Overall, the constant theme I noticed among these nudges is that firms want to keep you in the store as long as possible and get the most expensive products in front of you when you are most vulnerable to make regrettable purchases. Not many people really need to buy the expensive batteries or gum at the register, yet many do. Checkout lines serve as a way to have a captive audience for sweet and sugary products or the $3 Coca-Cola in the fridge. Everything down to the music is there for a specific reason.

Lee: You have earned the black belt in supermarket nudges.

Let me add to your list three nudges at Kroger, where I shop.

1. With few exceptions, Kroger does not put pale and skinny organic apples ($1.00 each) side by side with shiny big GMO apples ($0.50) each. I observe the same nudge in the meat section. The organics and inorganics are always displayed separately, often as far from each other as possible. That way, shoppers cannot easily compare prices and get discouraged by the much higher prices on organics.

2. Items with later expiration dates are always in the back or under the pile. You must make extra effort and take extra time to find them.
3. The bathrooms are all the way in the back and totally invisible. That is a negative nudge.

The bottom line is that, when I come out of the supermarket, the items in my cart are never exactly what I wrote down on the shopping list before I went in. For sure, the store manager is still disappointed at me, because I like to find and resist nudges. So exactly what does the stuff in my cart represent? I say that it is a compromise between the nudge-fighter in me and the nudge-maker in the store manager.

Further Readings

Schwartz, Elaine. "Six Facts About How Supermarkets Influence What We Buy." *Econlife*, 2 December 2018: https://econlife.com/2018/12/six-facts-about-supermarket-shopping/.

Thaler, Richard H., and Cass R. Sunstein. *Nudge: Improving Decisions About Health, Wealth, and Happiness*, Penguin, New York, 2009.

CONVERSATION 25

Demand Nudges: Wanna Health and/or Funeral Insurance?

Prompt I am considering two insurance policies: health and funeral. I met insurance agent David for both insurances. I told David that I have a "pre-condition": lung cancer. I also told him that I am on an experimental drug for the cancer. David said he knew the drug. So, we discussed the health insurance first and then the funeral insurance. I took some notes. I am looking at the notes and I am confused. David made two statements, one while we were talking about health insurance and the other while we were talking about funeral insurance.

Statement 1: "There is 80% chance that the drug you are taking will work, and you will live."

Statement 2: "There is 20% chance that the drug you are taking will not work, and you will die."

I don't remember which statement David made for what insurance. Help me out.

Keathley: It is likely that David made statement 1, "There is an 80% chance that the drug you are taking will work, and you will live," about the health insurance policy. He did this to frame your outlook in a positive way so as to encourage you to purchase the health insurance. When told that there is an 80% chance you will need something, you may round that up to 100% in your head and make the purchase. If he made statement 2 about the health insurance, you would be less likely to buy it because it highlights the death scene and that is a turnoff.

L. W. Lee and A. Keathley, *45 Conversations About Behavioral Economics*, https://doi.org/10.1007/978-3-031-05046-6_25

David likely used statement 2, "There is a 20% chance that the drug you are taking will not work, and you will die," about the funeral insurance. The funeral insurance sale is tougher for him because there is only a 20% chance that you will need to use it. If he had said, "There is an 80% chance that the drug you are taking will work, and you will not die," you would likely hear the statement as discouraging you from buying the funeral insurance. As someone who simply wants to make sale, David has framed each policy in such a way that someone not thinking very hard would instinctively want to purchase both policies. If he had used these statements incorrectly, you would have walked out with just one policy, or in his worst case scenario, neither.

This is very similar to the classic framing found on either yogurt or meat products. Producers know that no consumer wants to purchase a yogurt that says "20% fat" on it. They know that, if instead they frame their yogurt as "80% fat free," they will be putting their product in a positive light. This happens because when the brain sees a high percentage it often rounds it up to certainty, and when our brain sees a small percentage, it rounds it down to zero. So, when a producer promotes a product, it will highlight the abundance of a good ingredient (80% protein) or, when there are multiple good ingredients, the scarcity of a bad ingredient (80% fat free).

This type of framing is seen in lots of products and used to great success.

Lee: Right. Framing is everywhere. We are not aware of it most of the time. And that is the time when framing is most effective. Here are more examples:

1. Prices are $0.99, $9.99, $99...; coupons are $1, $10, $100....
2. Six chairs are for sale. The sale sign says: "Buy 3, Get 3 FREE!"

There is something about the word "free" that triggers the buy impulse.

Keathley: Getting things free to me indicates low quality. Before I buy these chairs, I will check out the quality of the chairs. I am also suspicious of big discount like "50% off." A big discount typically makes me think that it is an overpriced product the seller is looking to move quickly.

Lee: Products may be divided into "experience goods" and "inspection goods." The "buy-one-get-one free" signs are more common among experience goods, while the "50% off" signs are more common among inspection goods.

Sellers also frame a product by designing the context of consumption. When a new movie like Spiderman comes out, it is shown in theatres rather than on TV or disks. Theatres are essentially places where people herd.

Keathley: I may be in the minority, but I would much rather watch Spiderman at home. However, it is fascinating how consumers are often willing to pay more for context. At home you can pause, rewind, change the movie for free, watch on a better screen, and other things. The only thing the theatre has going for it is the social aspect.

Further Readings

Altman, Morris. *Behavioral Economics for Dummies*, John Wiley & Sons Canada, 2012.

Boyce, Paul. "Framing Effect Definition." *BoyceWire*, 8 February 2021: https://boycewire.com/framing-effect-definition-and-examples/.

CONVERSATION 26

Demand Norms: Picking College and Major

Prompt Norms, culture, peer pressure, and gender are parts of choice architecture. Let's talk about how they have played roles in our choices of college and major.

Keathley: Norms, culture, peer pressure, and gender have made a bigger impact on my decisions than I had ever before thought. Before even graduating middle school, I knew I was going to college. I have always been in private Catholic schools, and they teach you from a very young age that the best way to be successful is to go to college. They also occasionally would talk about trade schools or the military, but college was at the top of their list. I had always wanted to go to college, but this institutional pressure cemented the idea in my head.

When I was attempting to select a college, my first and foremost concern was price and quality of education. I wanted to go to a school that was large and had a reputation for being at least a decent school. I knew that I had no chance of going to an ivy league school, not because of lack of drive or motivation, but because of my test scores lying slightly below what they would accept and the astronomical price difference. However, after considering these factors, I still found more than one school on my list. This is where I began to be influenced by norms, culture, peer pressure, and gender.

L. W. Lee and A. Keathley, *45 Conversations About Behavioral Economics*, https://doi.org/10.1007/978-3-031-05046-6_26

My mother nudged me to go to Wayne State University because it is where she went to school. When talking to her about my college decision, I would often hear "why don't you just go to Wayne State; that is where I went and I'm successful." At the same time, I was nudged by societal pressure to go off to college and get the "college experience." This nudge was not effective on me because I understand that you do not have to live at a school to have fun and having fun at the cost of decades of debt is not a good decision. Today I don't look at these pressures in the negative light; I think they are beneficial to my decision making. They helped to provide context for deciding where to go to school.

The final thing that influenced my college decision was the city. Growing up just south of Detroit, I had always heard "Don't go there, you'll get shot." (Digression: I do not think that is the right thing to tell a 5 year old.) Eventually, as I grew up, I started to venture into the city for sporting events. Every time I went, I would feel less and less afraid to be there. At my first hockey game, I looked over my shoulder constantly and was terrified to walk to my car even with an enormous group of people. However, as the years went on and I did not get shot, mugged, or any of the other things I was told about Detroit, I began to love being downtown. I slowly ventured out farther and farther, and then started going to the city alone. By the time I was graduating high school I had been in the city enough to really understand it for what it was. I wanted to learn more and to experience more of what Detroit had to offer. So, what started out as a negative nudge changed as I grew older and became a driving factor in why I chose Wayne State.

As for my major, I have always wanted to study economics. Before I even knew what it really was, I was drawn to it for some reason. I distinctly remember playing videogames when I was young, and my favorite part of the game was taking all of the loot that I found and going from store to store to see where I could get the most money for it. I'm not sure how I translated this to economics, but I felt like the slickest businessman that any 10 year old could possibly be. However, the most profound and obvious societal nudge toward economics for me was the 2008 recession. The recession hit my family hard. My father lost his job, and it was just not a good time for us. When we started to do better, I wanted to know what happened and why life had got so bad. One day I watched the movie "The Big Short," and that was it. I was obsessed. I wanted to know everything there was about the recession. It was a subject that hit close to home. This interest gradually led me down the rabbit hole of politics. Politics and economics are intertwined quite well, and that is where my major is at this time.

Overall, I would say that these pressures have been a positive rather than a negative. I could not imagine attending another school or studying any other subject. For now, I feel that I am right where I am supposed to be. If my family was never hit by the recession, or my school did not push me to do well and go to college, I certainly would not be where I am today.

Lee: Your story makes me mull over my own experience with norms and cultures once again. I have lived in three countries and I don't know how many cultures. I grew up in Taiwan. As a teenager, I never seriously questioned if I wanted to go to college. The alternative was military service, followed perhaps by small business. Nobody I knew wanted to do that. So, I followed them, and they probably followed me.

As to my major, the decision was even easier: I left it to my mom. She was a pediatrician. I don't have to tell you what major she chose for me. As it turned out, fate intervened during my freshman year in medical school. I had to drop out and move with the family to New York City.

In New York City, I felt rootless, even "cultureless." Still, I did not become an entirely free spirit. Following a neighbor's tip, I checked into a college a few blocks down the street. It was a city college by the name of Queens College, and it was tuition free at that time. So it was a total no-brainer. A few years later, just when I was wondering about what to do next, fate intervened again. The Vietnam War broke out and I got a draft number. My choices were drastically reduced to one: graduate school. Long story short, the war nudged me into graduate studies.

As to how I ended up doing economics, it was an odyssey involving clashes among norms, cultures, peer pressure, luck, and a dash of free will. For sure, I did not pick economics by sitting down and solving the problem of maximizing a utility function under a budget constraint.

Further Readings

Teraji, Shinji. *Evolving Norms: Cognitive Perspectives in Economics*, Palgrave Macmillan, US, 2016.

Wexler, Ellen. "Geography Matters." *Inside Higher Ed*, 3 February 2016. https://www.insidehighered.com/news/2016/02/03/when-students-enroll-college-geography-matters-more-policy-makers-think.

Demand Norms: Keep and Return Equilibriums

Prompt People do different things about money found on the street. In some societies, the norm is: "Return it to its rightful owner." In other societies, the norm is: "Keep it; it is your good luck." Both norms are sustainable equilibriums; however, a society is better off in the "return" equilibrium than in the "keep" equilibrium. How does a society in the "keep" equilibrium move to the "return" equilibrium?

Keathley: In a society where the norm is "keep" rather than "return," everyone is better off being a keeper. A lone returner in a world of keepers is simply a sucker.

As to how to change a society from keepers to returners, my first thought was that the society institutes a reward policy. Under this policy, anyone who returned money or other things of value found on the street to the rightful owner would receive a reward. However, this policy will be tricky to design and implement. If the reward is made to be a sizable one, there will be fraud through choreographed "returns." This would be an expensive government program that would no doubt increase the amount of returns but would not be efficient in the slightest. On the other hand, if the reward is tiny, then no one would bother to return lost money.

My next thought was to create a government ad campaign. If the government spent a decent amount advertising the benefits of a society where the vast majority of people are returners, there would be an uptick

L. W. Lee and A. Keathley, *45 Conversations About Behavioral Economics*, https://doi.org/10.1007/978-3-031-05046-6_27

in returns. We have seen how successful governmental ad campaigns have been in discouraging smoking cigarettes in everyday life.

I believe in the power of advertising in changing a society's norms. Advertising against keeping money found on the street will not have the same speedy success that anti-smoking commercials did because keeping lost money does not cause life threatening cancer. However, the impact could grow over time. Parents who have seen these ads will pass the messages on to their kids, and so on and so on. Sooner or later, returners will drive out keepers. A similar transition can be found in the switch in "America's past time" from baseball to football. As generations are exposed to watching football rather than baseball, the number of dedicated baseball watchers slowly declines. There will always be baseball fans and there will always be keepers, but actions can be taken to minimize behavior that society no longer deems acceptable.

Lee: Both reward program and advertising campaign make sense.

Here I want to bring up a necessary condition for a successful change in norm: It requires both carrots and sticks. A norm change requires that society reach an agreement which is implicitly encoded in ethics or explicitly encoded in laws. For an agreement to succeed, there must be punishment for violations. In a society with the return norm, a keeper will face hostilities. The keeper may be shamed, shunned, fined, beaten, or jailed by returners. In the end, the keeper will learn the lesson that it is a bad idea to be a keeper among returners.

We pass laws because voluntary transition from a bad equilibrium to a good equilibrium is difficult or impossible. All laws have teeth.

Keathley: Still, I wonder how a keep equilibrium gets started. Could it be that societal inequality and monetary instability promote the keep mentality?

Lee: I guess the answer can be any of the following: history of the group, the emergence of religion, a new leader, war, famine, and drought. That is, I don't know.

I should mention that we started this conversation before we knew that others had done research on it already (Cohn et al. 2019). Thanks to a reviewer for the reference.

Reference

Cohn, Alain, Michel Marechal, David Tannenbaum, and Christian Zund. "Civic Honesty around the Globe." *Science*, 5 July 2019, pp. 70–73.

Further Readings

Angner, Erik. *A Course in Behavioral Economics*, Palgrave Macmillan, New York, NY, 2012.

Denworth, Lydia. "'Missing' Wallets with More Cash Are More Likely to Be Returned." *Scientific American*, 20 June 2019: https://www.scientificamerican.com/article/missing-wallets-with-more-cash-are-more-likely-to-be-returned/.

Kennedy, Merrit. "What Dropping 17,000 Wallets Around The World Can Teach Us About Honesty." *NPR*, 20 June 2019: https://www.npr.org/2019/06/20/734141432/what-dropping-17-000-wallets-around-the-globe-can-teach-us-about-honesty.

CONVERSATION 28

Demand Bubbles: Tulip and Other Famous Bubbles

Prompt Look up some "famous market bubbles" and talk about the one that strikes you most.

Keathley: Whenever I think about economic bubbles, the first that comes to my mind is the South Sea bubble. I am not sure if it is the convoluted nature of the scheme, or the fact that it happened in such a different world, or something else, but I am always drawn back to eighteenth-century Britain and John Blunt. The story goes something like this. Britain was in a bad way financially at that point in the eighteenth century and turned to John Blunt, secretary of the Hollow Sword Blade company for help. (Yes, I too see the irony is someone named Blunt running a sword company.) Together the British treasury and Blunt created a trading company similar to the famous East India Company and transferred all of Britain's massive debts to this new South Sea Company. Holders of the government debt were only willing to take this deal if they thought the company would be profitable enough to make it worth giving up the high interest rate the government was already paying them. This was achieved by a grant of monopoly on trading in the South Seas. The grant was made in spite of the fact that Spain, not Britain, owned the South Sea ports.

Here we can see the seeds of a speculation bubble being sewn. Rather than making hundreds of yearly voyages like the East India Company, Blunt was permitted by Spain to make only one voyage. Blunt decided

L. W. Lee and A. Keathley, *45 Conversations About Behavioral Economics*, https://doi.org/10.1007/978-3-031-05046-6_28

he would make it his mission to raise the stock price of South Sea Company by any means necessary. He forgave interest payments owed by the government in exchange for the ability to issue an equal number of shares in his company. They would go on to issue over 10 million shares in this company.

Over time, the value of these shares skyrocketed as the King of England and Blunt said and did whatever it took to make the price go up. The shares in the company got so high that they officially made a profit. They paid off the entire debt Britain had accrued over a century-long war and officially were in the green. People continued to trade government debt for shares at the price set by parliament and then sell the shares on the open market for massive profits. Eventually, the company took on 31 million pounds in new government debt, and at this point, a single dollar increase in the stock price translated to millions of profit in today's money. Blunt resorted to bribing parliament and giving them free shares in order for them to let him take on this debt. This company quickly resembled a Ponzi scheme that required constant growth to stay afloat. He even let people purchase shares with payment plans and offered loans that were conditioned to be only used for purchasing new shares.

As the Blunt scheme hit its high point, they had an evaluation greater than all the money in the British economy then. It is easy to forget in all this talk about share price and price manipulation that it was a trading company. Moreover, the company had never actually gone out and made any profits.

Like all bubbles, this bubble collapsed under its own weight. People finally caught wind of the Blunt scheme and the share price collapsed from $1000 to $150 in three weeks. Following the company's collapse many politicians had to resign in disgrace and thousands of people's life savings were gone. This bubble is a cautionary tale about what happens when governments search for a quick solution to a century-long money problem and what happens when politicians are regulating financial vehicles to which they are personally attached.

By the way, I watched a documentary on the South Sea bubble (*Extra-Credits*). It consists of five episodes. I learned a lot from them. The basic lesson is that, if a business is giving you money on the condition that you turn around and give it back to them in exchange for shares in their company, run.

Lee: Great pick of bubble. From what you are telling me, the South Sea Bubble does look like a Ponzi scheme. As Shiller (2005) puts it, market bubbles are "naturally occurring Ponzi processes." They all are created and sustained by the stories people tell each other.

Here is a true story about making bubble. One day I went to an ethnic food festival. There were dozens and dozens of food stands, each offering something special. I had no idea what the vendors were offering, so I just joined the longest line in the sandwich section, then the longest line in the desert section, then the longest line in the beverage section. Each time I joined a line, I noticed that someone would follow me, and others would appear out of nowhere to join the line as well. A line could grow quickly. I heard people in front of me and behind me asking each other about the food they were lining up for. Few had a clue. They joined the line for the same reason that I joined the line: It was the longest line in that section of the compound. I also remember the neighboring vendor well. He got no customer at all, and was pacing back and forth in front of his stand to attract attention. It was all to no avail. I felt guilty.

Keathley: I think the food festival story is very helpful for understanding how herd behavior can cause bubbles.

References

"England: South Sea Bubble—The Sharp Mind of John Blunt—Extra History - #1." *YouTube*, uploaded by *ExtraCredits*, 28 February 2015: https://www.youtube.com/watch?v=k1kndKWJKB8&t=46s.

"England: South Sea Bubble—The Sharp Mind of John Blunt—Extra History - #2." *YouTube*, uploaded by *ExtraCredits*, 14 March 2015: https://www.youtube.com/watch?v=Fsk6oZm1EEA.

"England: South Sea Bubble—The Sharp Mind of John Blunt—Extra History—#3." *YouTube*, uploaded by *ExtraCredits*, 28 March 2015: https://www.youtube.com/watch?v=1vcF5rebN20.

"England: South Sea Bubble—The Sharp Mind of John Blunt—Extra History—#4." *YouTube*, uploaded by *ExtraCredits*, 11 April 2015: https://www.youtube.com/watch?v=SIlnsP6AjP8.

"England: South Sea Bubble—The Sharp Mind of John Blunt—Extra History—#5." *YouTube*, uploaded by *ExtraCredits*, 28 March 2015: https://www.youtube.com/watch?v=a_1IpUCUuVc.

Shiller, Robert. *Irrational Exuberance*, 2nd edition, Princeton University Press, Princeton, New Jersey, 2005.

Further Readings

Mackay, Charles. *Memoirs of Extraordinary Popular Delusions and the Madness of Crowds*, Richard Bentley, New Burlington Street, London, 1841 (Republished by L. C. Page and Company, Boston, 1932).

Shiller, Robert. *Irrational Exuberance*, 2nd edition, Princeton University Press, Princeton, New Jersey, 2005.

CONVERSATION 29

Demand Bubbles: Demand by Robots

Prompt Demand is not just a biological thing anymore. Demand comes from robots as well. For example, robots—known collectively as AI or algorithms—buy and sell in the stock market. I wonder if robot traders have played a role in the stock market swings during the Covid-19 pandemic.

Keathley: It is no secret that the stock market did not take Covid-19 kindly in the beginning. On March 16, 2020, the Dow Jones fell 13%, which was the largest single day fall since the 1980s.

Technology has definitely advanced since the 1980s, and moved in on a previously human only gig, stock trading. Machine trading takes an AI or a machine learning algorithm and gives it the power to trade stocks and their derivatives. Machines can make these transactions instantly. However, these machines are missing certain fail safes. That has serious consequences for the firms that employ them.

To understand this topic better, I read an article by Will Knight (2020). He talks about how several trading companies that rely on algorithms and AI to make their trades lost between 9 and 21% of their value in March 2020. The most alarming thing that I took from this article was that MIT Professor Andrew Lo said that this crash was similar to the 2007 crash but faster. This speed is likely due to the increase in machine trading and the larger portfolios that algorithms manage.

L. W. Lee and A. Keathley, *45 Conversations About Behavioral Economics*, https://doi.org/10.1007/978-3-031-05046-6_29

Knight (2020) quotes the chairman at the quant fund DE Shaw, Ray Dalio, as saying that their algorithms were not equipped to deal with such a volatile market as we experienced in March 2020. Human decisions like hoarding toilet paper and bottled water are the kind of volatility that these AI models could not predict. Dalio goes on to say that the firms with the more complex algorithms seemed to do more poorly as their AI tried to align its trading strategy with the erratic behavior of humans. The more complex the algorithms and the more rigid the trading parameters in them, the worse they did. Simply put, these robots were trained for normal time, not a once-in-a-century crisis.

Here, we see the limitations of current robot traders. Since they do not know how to deal with large swings in the market, they failed during chaos. However, Knight sees hope. He mentions that some firms that employ machine trading profited and are continuing to use new forms of data to prepare these machines for illogical human behavior in desperate situations.

This conversation serves as a great reminder of how far we still have to go with AI in order to make it understand human behavior. I think that human beings will always find a way to tank the market. Robots need to know that.

Lee: Your take on machine trading is fair and balanced. It is making me think about the difference between machine trading and human trading.

In the final analysis, algorithms are heuristics. However, robot traders' heuristics are more similar than human traders' heuristics. As a result, robot traders are more inclined to herd. A few human traders knock down a domino or two. Robot traders see it, and they start knocking down more. The market begins to swing.

I am not surprised that robot traders are beginning to learn behavioral economics. It is about time. But economists also need to build AI into their models of decision making. Herbert Simon (1982) was an early advocate of the integration of economics and AI. His work on mental models is interdisciplinary of the highest order. He was a Professor of Computer Science and Psychology and winner of a Nobel Prize in, well, economics. Simon inspired me to look into what is going on in a human or animal head. I regret that I never got around to studying AI, or what is going on in a robot's head.

Meanwhile, we can thank robot traders for more market bubbles, crashes, and maniacs to come.

References

Knight, Will. "Even the Best AI Models Are No Match for the Coronavirus." *Wired*, 19 July 2020: www.wired.com/story/best-ai-models-no-match-coronavirus/.

Simon, Herbert. *Behavioral Economics and Business Organization*, volume 2 of *Models of Bounded Rationality* (three-volume series), The MIT Press, Cambridge, Massachusetts, 1982.

Further Readings

Collins, Jason. "Simple Heuristics That Make Algorithms Smart." *Behavioral Scientist*, 12 December 2018: https://behavioralscientist.org/simple-heuristics-that-make-algorithms-smart/.

PART III

Market

We have met a lot of buyers and sellers by now. There are still more people to meet. They are third parties in transactions; nonetheless, they are fully engaged in the functioning of the marketplace. Here is a roster of them:

A. Regulators
B. Trustbusters
C. Scammers
D. Creative Destructors
E. Raiders

(We have 10 conversations about them.)

We shall recognize them one at a time. We talk about what they each bring to or take away from the market. By the end of our conversations, you will agree with us on one thing: They are a natural part of the market ecosystem.

Regulators: Truth in Labeling

Prompt Information is never perfect. That is why there are labels. But labels can be misleading and false. That is why there are people who offer to certify the accuracy of claims on labels. For each of the three products below, identify the major certifiers.

a. corporate bonds
b. organic food
c. social media messages

Keathley: Labelling can shape how products are perceived by consumers, and that can influence what gets purchased. True or false, information on a label is part of the economy. First, with corporate bonds, these are regulated by both public and private agents. The US Securities and Exchange Commission (SEC) is the main public agent. As to private agents, Paddy Hirsch (2012, pp. 160–161) points out that there are 3 of them in the United States: Fitch Ratings, Moody's Investor Service, and Standard and Poor's. This is not ideal because in an industry with such a small number of rating agents, bond sellers can shop around and look where they can get the most favorable rating. This leads to competition among these 3 agencies, resulting in false ratings in order to get more business (Hirsch 2012, p. 191).

L. W. Lee and A. Keathley, *45 Conversations About Behavioral Economics*, https://doi.org/10.1007/978-3-031-05046-6_30

As for organic foods, this responsibility rests solely on two public agencies: The National Organic Project (NOP) and the United States Department of Agriculture (USDA). Both are divisions of the Food and Drug Administration (FDA). Both are focused on the term "organic" on a food label; they do not regulate products that want to use similar terms like "healthy" or "natural" on their product labels.

Lastly, social media companies are regulated by the Federal Communications Commission. However, this federal regulator has essentially no power to dictate what can and cannot be said on these sites. This power is left completely up to the companies that run the social media pages. Historically, social media have allowed just about anything to be posted on their sites because of the first amendment. As long as they are not filtering what can and cannot be posted on their website, these companies are not liable for what individual users post. However, as of late there have been signs of change. Social media companies have started to delete information about the Covid-19 pandemic, voter registration, absentee voting, and voting by mail information that they deem to be false. Also, they have been putting notices under posts that they do not want to delete (like some from a U.S. President). It seems as if they do want to make sure that their users are getting mostly accurate information.

Lee: Our conversation here is meant to spotlight a fact of life: what you see often is not what you get.

Fraud is everywhere in modern markets. Economists as a whole, however, have remained willfully blind to the prevalence of fraud; they sweep fraud under the "market imperfection" carpet. When was the last time you studied fraud in an economics course? George Akerlof and Robert Shiller (2015) were so bothered by this willful blindness that they wrote an entire book to call attention to "phishing for phools" in the economy. (We should lend them our ears as they both have the Nobel Prize in economics under their belts.)

Many economists think (at least say) that consumers are sovereign. I say not so fast. Consumers don't always get to decide what are produced; rather, they get to buy what producers decide to produce and want them to buy. As Komlos (2019) puts it, consumers are producers' Pavlov dogs.

How about the regulators that you have identified in bonds, organic food, and social media? Sorry, they are not any more immune to manipulation by producers. Regulators are humans, too: they are driven by self-interest. Producers know that, and they are constantly trying to capture the regulators. As you have mentioned, "regulatory capture" is endemic in the bond rating circle.

Court judges, who are part of the network of regulators, are not immune to phishing and capture. Judges are humans, too. They compete for hearings. The result is "forum selling" (Bechtold et al. 2019).

Keathley: In a way this is a market working exactly as it should: producers competing for buyers of their products. However, do we really want bond rating to be a private product, rather than a public service? This seems like a big moral hazard. Why don't governmental bodies rate bonds?

Lee: Probably for the same reason why government bodies don't rate stocks.

References

Akerlof, George, and Robert Shiller. *Phishing for Phools*, Princeton University Press, Princeton, New Jersey, 2015.

Bechtold, Stefan, Jens Frankenreiter, and Daniel Klerman. "Forum Selling Abroad," *Southern California Law Review*, 92(3), 2019, pp. 487–559.

Hirsch, Paddy. *Man vs Markets*. HarperCollins Publishers, New York, NY, 2012, pp. 160–161.

Komlos, John. *Foundations of Real-World Economics: What Every Economics Student Needs to Know*, 2nd ed., Routledge, Taylor and Francis, 2019.

Further Readings

Akerlof, George, and Robert Shiller. *Phishing for Phools*, Princeton University Press, Princeton, New Jersey, 2015.

Jacobs, Andrew. "Lawsuits Over 'Misleading' Food Labels Surge as Groups Cite Lax U.S. Oversight." *The New York Times*, 7 September 2021: https://www.nytimes.com/2021/09/07/science/food-labels-lawsuits.html.

Suneson, Grant, and John Harrington. "What Products Were Among Those Marketed with the Most Outrageous Claims of All Time?" *USA Today*, 9 June 2020: https://www.usatoday.com/story/money/2020/06/09/39-most-outrageous-false-product-claims-of-all-time/111913486/.

CONVERSATION 31

Regulators: Regulation, Regulation Everywhere

Prompt All markets are regulated. For each of the markets below, identify the nature of regulation on either the buyer or the seller or both:

a. automobile
b. house
c. alcohol
d. cow milk
e. heroin

Keathley: In automobile market, a majority of the regulations fall on sellers. New automobiles must meet safety and environmental standards set by the National Highway Traffic Safety Administration (NHTSA) and the Environmental Protection Agency (EPA). NHTSA requires that certain safety mechanisms are put into cars, and that these safety mechanisms are effective. As a result, automobiles are drastically safer, but also cost more. Imagine cars that did not have air bags, seat belts, anti-lock brakes, or shatterproof windshields. These cars would be cheaper but much less safe. I think most people agree that these regulations are beneficial to society. At the same time, EPA requires different types of cars to hit certain fuel efficiency standards and certain pollution emission levels. As anyone who has ever had to replace a catalytic convertor can attest, these emission regulation parts are not cheap. (A month ago, someone stole

L. W. Lee and A. Keathley, *45 Conversations About Behavioral Economics*, https://doi.org/10.1007/978-3-031-05046-6_31

the catalytic convertor on my car.) The car buyer is also regulated but in much less detail. Every state requires a driver to have a license and car registrations. All but two states require the driver to have car insurance.

Many government agencies have their hands in housing. The first agency that comes to mind is the Department of Housing and Urban Development. It enforces things like the fair housing act and other anti-discriminatory statutes. It tries to make housing affordable through subsidies and price control. This is much more common as a state regulation in the nation's largest cities. As for safety, each state regulates the quality of housing through building codes. Lastly, Freddie Mac, Fannie Mae, Ginnie Mae have a big impact in the mortgage market. That makes them regulators of housing, too.

As to alcohol, The Department of Treasury's Alcohol and Tobacco Tax and Trade Bureau (TTB) handles a lot of the traditional regulation. It monitors the production and sale of alcohol products to make sure that they are safe. It makes sure that alcohol products are labeled correctly. A tequila with a label claiming 100% agave must be 100% agave. TTB collects the excise taxes that alcohol generates. It regulates the marketing of alcohol. It makes sure that labels on alcoholic beverages properly warn buyers the dangers of alcohol. Buyers of alcohol also face regulation. The most obvious is an age requirement. The national minimum age to purchase and consume alcohol legally is 21. Other common regulations are minimum price levels set by the states to discourage consumption, licenses to sell certain kinds of alcohol at bars and restaurants, and restricted store hours for the sale of alcoholic beverages. Many of us think that alcohol is regulated by the Bureau of Alcohol, Tobacco, and Firearms, but this agency is more concerned with alcohol trafficking.

Milk and other dairy products are regulated by the Food and Drug Administration (FDA). This agency requires milk to be pasteurized so that outbreaks of disease related to spoiled milk do not occur. Lots of states regulate the price of milk directly to help their dairy industry. For example, Pennsylvania has a price floor to keep milk prices high in their state. As for the buyer of milk, there seem to be no regulations.

Heroin is an illicit drug. It is outright banned by the federal government for production, possession, sale, or consumption. Federal laws threaten buyers and sellers with jail time and fines. To evade penalties, buyers and sellers have gone underground. The consumers of heroin incur large indirect cost for participating in this market. For example, take a look at the recent outbreak of heroin spiked with fentanyl.

Lee: Nice job. The closer we look, the more regulations we see in any market. Regulations are always in the DNA of a market. We should throw models of "free market" out of the window.

Before we move on, I want to quickly mention a couple points about regulations. First, regulations don't all have to be public policies (emphasis on "public"). When we look closely, all markets have private regulations as well. American Medical Association (AMA) is an example of private regulation. Dairy Farmers of America (DFA) is another example. So, between public and private regulations, markets are choke-full of them; markets are not free.

My second point is that regulation is not Band-Aid; regulation is chemo. Regulation changes the body of the market by changing how internal organs of the market work. Here is a story about that. Some years ago I got interested in illicit drug markets (Lee 1993). The more I studied them, the more intrigued I became. I felt as if I was looking at another universe. Buyers of crack cocaine face risks of arrest and fine and robbery each time they make a purchase, so they make fewer purchases, but buy a greater quantity at each purchase. The result is that a user needs to maintain an inventory of crack cocaine, which exposes the user to greater risks of possession penalty and overdose. Users also form groups when they do cocaine. By watching over each other, they reduce the risk of overdose. But a group attracts attention more easily than a solitary user. Regulation of cocaine has changed the supply side just as profoundly. Sellers have moved underground. The supply chain has become long, thin, loose, and international. The purity of the drug has gone down. Competition has become, literally, cut-throat.

Keathley: I appreciate your willingness to throw out the textbook concept of a "free market." After hearing lots and lots about the requirement for a free market (largely from conservative political talk radio that I listen to occasionally), it is refreshing to hear someone in academia confirm my idea that a truly free market does not exist. I am not a radical, I understand that bad regulation can definitely stifle markets, but I do reject the popular notion "any regulation is bad regulation." The sooner politicians and citizens understand that regulations will always be in markets in some way, the sooner we can get to thinking about better solutions to our problems.

Reference

Lee, Li Way. "Would Harassing Drug Users Work?" *Journal of Political Economy*, 101, October 1993, pp. 939–959.

Further Readings

Goetz, Gretchen. "Who Inspects What? A Food Safety Scramble." *Food Safety News*, 16 December 2010.

Lee, Li Way. "A Theory of Just Regulation." *American Economic Review*, December 1980, 848–862.

CONVERSATION 32

Trustbusters: DuPont and GM then

Prompt Read Section 1 and Section 2 of the antitrust law Sherman Act. Then summarize two cases:

a. U.S. v General Motors, 1966
b. U.S. v E. I. DuPont, 1956

Keathley: The GM case is the first that I learned about antitrust. I looked up *Justia*. This case was about how the Supreme Court handled an appeal by the U.S. government against three Chevrolet dealer associations in Los Angeles, California. The government appealed because a lower court found that the GM dealers were not in violation of Section 1 of the Sherman Act. This law deals with conspiracies to prevent trade. The government accused General Motors of preventing the sale of new Chevrolets through "discount houses" and "referral services." The problem was not that one dealer decided not to move cars through a discount seller, but rather that many dealers had agreed to prevent the discount houses in the Los Angeles area from getting new Chevrolet cars. The associations also made dealers that had already sold cars to discount sellers buy the cars back. This limited price competition. The lower court dismissed this suit because no formal written agreement was made among the dealers. However, the US Supreme court overruled this

L. W. Lee and A. Keathley, *45 Conversations About Behavioral Economics*, https://doi.org/10.1007/978-3-031-05046-6_32

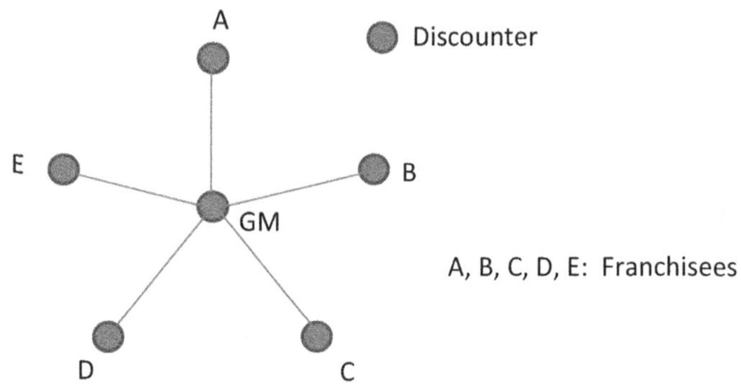

Fig. 32.1 A GM franchise problem

decision, on the ground that a written agreement was not required to deem coordinated actions as a conspiracy.

To learn about the DuPont case, I looked up *LexusNexis* and *Justia*. In 1955, the federal government sued the DuPont company. The government alleged that DuPont was in violation of Section 2 of the Sherman Act for producing 75% of all the cellophane that was sold in the United States. The government accused DuPont of having an illegal monopoly over cellophane production. However, the district court did not side with the federal government. The court ruled on behalf of DuPont and said that it did not have a monopoly because it didn't have the ability to control prices in the flexible packaging materials market. Cellophane made up only 20% of all flexible packaging materials sold. That was not enough for DuPont to have monopoly in that market. The government appealed this decision, but the Supreme Court confirmed the decision.

Lee: I learned these cases first from Stelzer (1986), which contains original but abbreviated decisions. Complete decisions would probably take days to read, not to mention digest.

You did a great job explaining the decision about GM. I understand the court's application of Section 1 there. But I see an unsolved puzzle: A franchise is a legal contract between the franchisor and franchisees. That is, a franchise system is a legal conspiracy. Figure 32.1 is a network picture of the GM franchise system in Los Angeles.

In a franchise agreement, the franchisor can legally require franchisees to follow four business practices:

- territorial/customer restrictions
- exclusive dealing
- resale price maintenance
- service specifications

I am not going into details about these business practices here. You can tell easily that they are designed to restrict competition among franchisees.

The problem that GM faced in L.A. was that discounters were getting around the customer restrictions. Dealer X, who knows better than take an order for 10 Chevys from the US Army or LA Police Department, wants to sell the 10 cars to a guy by the name of Joe Smith. What is wrong with that? Why would dealer X bother to find out why Joe Smith wants 10 cars?...But of course dealer X knows that Joe Smith will resell the cars to people living in other dealers' prescribed territories. Joe Smith is just a reseller trying to make a living. He is not bound by any of the clauses in a GM franchisee agreement. He sells below the sticker price. He does not provide pre-sale and after-sale service. He has no showroom. He does not offer test drives. His customers can get all these services free from Chevy dealers.

Discounters are the bane of a franchise system. But the Supreme Court in the GM case did not see them that way. Any agreement between GM and franchisees to exclude discounters is a conspiracy, and all conspiracies in commerce are per se illegal, the court says. Section 1 of Sherman Act does not require a showing of bad consequences of an agreement; it requires only proof of an agreement. In the GM case, no one denies that there was an agreement, tacit or explicit, about the exclusion of buyers like discounters.

Antitrust issues are complex, and judges so far are humans. It is no wonder that per se illegality has been a fast-and-frugal antitrust heuristic. Indeed, a literature has emerged that examines how antitrust judges make decisions. It is known as behavioral antitrust.

The DuPont case is another favorite of mine. The case highlights the concept of "relevant market." From the outset, Justice Reed grappled with the question of monopolization, which is what Section 2 of Sherman prohibits. He asked whether, from the users' point of view, cellophane was a product all by itself or just one of several products that are substitutable.

In Fig. 32.2, cellophane is not part of another market. In that case, DuPont must have monopolized, as no one who has monopoly does not

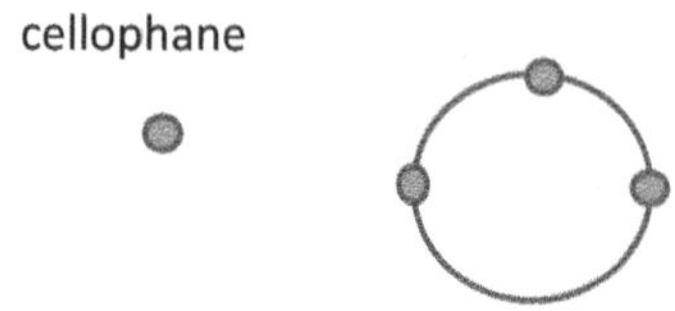

Fig. 32.2 Cellophane is a monopoly

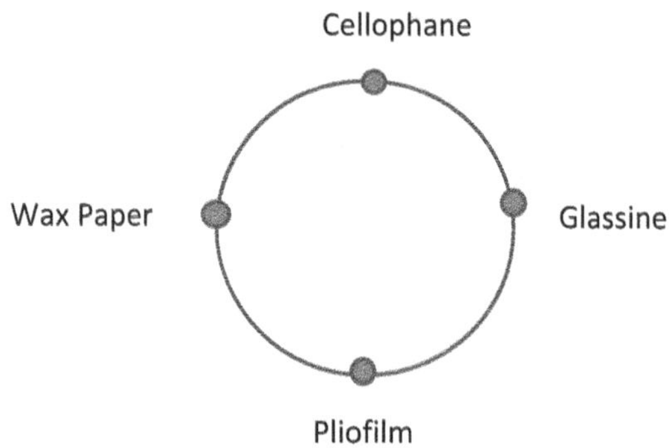

Fig. 32.3 Cellophane is not a monopoly

monopolize. DuPont would have to be dealt with under Section 2 of Sherman.

In Fig. 32.3, cellophane is one of four flexible packaging materials. Each of the four commands a share of the market. DuPont could not have monopolized.

But which is cellophane's "relevant market"? Fig. 32.2 or Fig. 32.3? Reasoning is required. This rule for the application of Section 2 of the Sherman Act is known as "rule of reason." You mention that he used survey to answer the question of relevant market. He asked a group of merchants what wrapping materials they were using. He asked them why they did not use cellophane. After the survey, he decided that cellophane was in competition with other wrapping materials. He would pick Fig. 32.3 as cellophane's relevant market. Oh, a body of research has developed from this case: The Cellophane Paradox. Check it out.

References

United States v. E. I. Du Pont De Nemours & Co. - 351 U.S. 377, 76 S. Ct. 994. *LexisNexis*, 1956a: www.lexisnexis.com/community/casebrief/p/casebrief-united-states-v-e-i-du-pont-de-nemours-co.

United States v. E. I. Du Pont De Nemours & Co., 351 U.S. 377. *Justia*, 1956a: http://supreme.justia.com/cases/federal/us/351/377/.

Stelzer, Irwin. *Selected Antitrust Cases: Landmark Decisions*, 7th edition, Irwin, Inc., Homewood, IL, 1986.

CONVERSATION 33

Trustbusters: Big Techs Now

Prompt In recent years, technology companies have come under antitrust scrutiny in a large part of the world. In the U.S., Facebook is the subject of a complaint filed by FTC (Federal Trade Commission). The complaint says that Facebook has been trying to stifle competition. Facebook's retort is: Competition with whom? FTC is struggling to respond. Let's talk about this case of "show me my relevant market."

Keathley: Believe it or not, as much as the phrase "big tech" gets used in our modern vocabulary, I had no idea about this case before this conversation. To catch up on the proceedings, I read one article from *The New York Times* (Kang 2021) and two articles from *NPR* (Bond 2020, 2021). (Full disclosure: Facebook helps fund *NPR*.)

Essentially, FTC (and 48 state Attorney Generals) claimed that Facebook had been "suppressing, neutralizing, and deterring serious competitive threats" in order to unfairly dominate the social media industry. They were pushing for a breakup of the company's assets on the ground that Facebook was an illegal monopoly. The FTC's case can be summed up by a 2008 quote from Facebook CEO, Mark Zuckerberg: "It is better to buy than compete" (Bond 2020). FTC thought that acquisitions of other large companies like WhatsApp and Instagram would make this case a slam dunk.

However, in June 2021, FTC got thrown a wrench and Facebook a bone. Federal Judge James Boasberg of the US District Court for the

L. W. Lee and A. Keathley, *45 Conversations About Behavioral Economics*, https://doi.org/10.1007/978-3-031-05046-6_33

District of Columbia threw out the complaints that FTC lobbied against the social media giant. His ruling left little to the imagination as he plainly said: "The FTC has failed to plead enough facts to plausibly establish a necessary element of all of its Section 2 claims — namely, that Facebook has monopoly power in the market for Personal Social Networking Services." However, this ruling was not the end of the road for this case, as the judge allowed FTC 30 days to come up with a new complaint that explains FTC's claim of a 60 plus% market share (Bond 2021).

I agree with you when you say that FTC is struggling to define the market that Facebook is in. This is evident even after a cursory glance at their latest complaint. The filing reiterates their original arguments but with much more in the department of data, examples, and statistics (Kang 2021). In the new filing, FTC works harder to define "Personal Social Networking Services" and how Facebook monopolizes it. For example, the agency sought to differentiate Facebook from what Facebook called its competitors (Twitter, YouTube, TikTok, and LinkedIn). FTC argued that, in regard to social networking, instant messaging and entertainment, Facebook's products were for "Personal Social Networking Services." That is different from more specific networking sites like LinkedIn. As for YouTube, TikTok, and Twitter, FTC argues that "those sites were typically created for the public and not directed at specific individuals in a social network" (Kang 2021).

The burden that FTC faces is to define what Facebook actually does as a business. FTC needs to define the relevant market that Facebook is allegedly monopolizing. FTC is working very hard to show that Facebook is the sole proprietor of services in its specific lane of social networking, but its new filing shows the difficulties it is having doing just that. Former FTC chairman under President George W Bush, Bill Kovacic, shares my worry. He said that "the case would face a long and steep challenge" (Kang 2021). I think FTC is going to continue to struggle in convincing a federal judge of the "60 plus percent" market share they claim Facebook has. As you say in your most recent book (Lee 2019, Chapter 4), the definition of a market is always subjective. Perhaps Facebook is 60 plus % of the "Personal Social Networking Service" market, or maybe it is 40% of the app market, or 10% of the internet market. Only a judge's opinion will decide.

Lee: Big technology companies have been on antitrust radars all over the world for several years. The European Union has been the most aggressive. It has been going after Google in particular. I have lost track of how many billions of euros it has fined Google for violations of EU antitrust laws. So far, EU prefers "behavioral remedies." A behavioral remedy means ordering a company to stop monopolizing, or a group of companies to stop merging and fixing price. Behavioral remedies often include big fines.

Breakup is the bigger threat. A breakup means taking a company like Amazon and slicing it into several "baby Amazons." The hope is that baby Amazons will then compete with each other. The U.S. has done company breakups. For example, the U.S. broke up American Telephone and Telegraph (AT&T).

Keathley: Has anyone tried to break up large banks? I see large banks getting larger and larger after 2008, and they scare me. If Citibank or JP Morgan Chase should fail, I'm not sure what would happen to the world.

Lee: U.S. v Philadelphia National Bank 1963 comes to mind. But that was not a case of breaking up a bank. It was a case of prohibiting the merger between two banks.

Don't hold your breath about the Facebook case. I bet it will take years before resolution. I know cases that took 10 years. Big technology companies all have very deep pockets. They can hire armies of attorneys and economists to fight in courts. Antitrust breakup has an extremely poor track record. I don't even remember the last breakup.

Keathley: Why is this? Is the law written poorly for modern times? Are courts reluctant to breakup firms? If so, why?

Lee: I would ask Tim Wu (2019). He is an advisor to President Biden, who may very well be asking him the same questions.

The biggest caveat about breakup is that it works only for a while. After the breakups, the baby Bells and the baby Standard Oils started to merge among themselves. Soon they reconstituted the DNAs of their parents. They merely have adopted different names, like Exxon-Mobil.

Meanwhile, there will be so much change in the economy as to render the original breakup obsolete.

References

Bond, Shannon. "'The Wrath of Mark': 4 Takeaways From The Government's Case Against Facebook." *NPR*, 11 December 2020.

Bond, Shannon. "Facebook Gets Reprieve As Court Throws Out Major Antitrust Complaints." *NPR*, 28 June 2021.

Kang, Cecilia. "U.S. Revives Facebook Suit, Adding Details to Back Claim of a Monopoly." *The New York Times*, 19 August 2021.
Lee, Li Way. *Industrial Organization: Minds, Bodies, and Epidemics*, Palgrave Macmillan, Switzerland, 2019.
Wu, Tim. *The Curse of Bigness: Antitrust in the New Gilded Age*, Columbia Global Reports, New York, NY, 2019.

Further readings

Feiner, Lauren. "States Bring a New Antitrust Suit Against Google Over Its Mobile App Store." *CNBC*, 7 July 2021.
Wu, Tim. *The Curse of Bigness: Antitrust in the New Gilded Age*, New York, NY 2019.

Scammers: Ponzi Scheme

Prompt Pick a "famous Ponzi scheme" and tell us about it. To find Ponzi schemes, will you be looking in large or small firms?

Keathley: In a Ponzi scheme, the operator simply pays original investors with the money that new investors contribute. The scheme operator is quite literally "robbing Peter to pay Paul." There is no Ponzi scheme more famous than the one operated by Bernie Madoff (*Wikipedia* 2020). His scheme lasted from the mid-60s up until 2008. When he was prosecuted, his scheme was worth over $64.8 billion based on the accounts of 4800 people. That is $13.5 million per account! His scheme started out with having backroom workers at his investment company creating false trading records about whatever stocks performed well that day. They were even so careless as to produce records saying trades happened on weekends and holidays when no actual trades took place. During his trial, he admitted that he put all of the money that investors gave him into a Chase bank savings account to generate steady but minimal returns. If any investor wanted money returned, he would simply withdraw whatever amount that the investor was supposed to have from the savings account and the investor would be none the wiser.

He was eventually caught after many other investment executives reported him to the SEC. Harry Markopoulos, a financial fraud investigator, claimed that, for Madoff to achieve the returns he claimed, he would have had to buy more options on the Chicago Board Options

L. W. Lee and A. Keathley, *45 Conversations About Behavioral Economics*, https://doi.org/10.1007/978-3-031-05046-6_34

Exchange than had ever existed. Madoff was convicted and sentenced to 150 years in federal prison. (He died in 2021.)

Large firms and Ponzi schemes can appear to be very similar except for one small detail. Ponzi schemes do not have any real product or source of income aside from the input of investors. Bernie Madoff had no way to fuel his scheme except for the recruitment of new investors. If Tyson Chicken suddenly could not find investors for a new adventure in space travel, they should still be able to pay their debtors in the new project by using profit from their chicken sales.

Lee: Now that you know so much about a Ponzi scheme, you may be wondering why I bring it up when we are talking about the architecture of market.

Well, my answer is that Ponzi schemes—or frauds, scams, whatever we call them—are inherent in all firms. They are like cancer cells. We all have got cancer cells more or less of one kind or the other. (Most of us do not know about them.) Ponzi schemes thrive in large, complex firms. That is because the best cover for a Ponzi scheme is complexity. Take a big organization like a national bank. It has hundreds of financial products. It processes billions of dollars of transactions every day. No one can account for all of the activities on its ledger. So, if one project is a Ponzi scheme, it will not raise suspicion right away. Indeed, with skillful obfuscation, it may never be revealed as a fraud.

Fraud and complexity feed on each other. Ponzi schemes make for complex organizations, which in turn encourage Ponzi schemes. Since bigness and complexity are two sides of the same coin, big organizations and fraud go hand in hand as well. Your example about Tyson Chicken says it all.

Reference

Wikipedia. "Bernie Madoff." *Wikimedia Foundation*, 8 September 2020: https://en.wikipedia.org/wiki/Bernie_Madoff.

Further Reading

Akerlof, George A., and Robert J. Shiller. *Phishing for Phools: The Economics of Manipulation and Deception*, Princeton University Press, 2015.

Scammers: Enron Scheme

Prompt A Ponzi scheme is like a rotten apple. If it sits alone, we can tell it by smelling and squeezing. But when it sits with other apples and fruits, we cannot pick it out easily. Take the firm Enron, which was found to have been a rotten apple. How was Enron able to get away with it for so long?

Keathley: To get a basic idea of what went down at Enron in 2001, I took a look around on the Wikipedia page "Enron scandal." (When a scandal has its own Wikipedia page, you know something seriously bad happened.) I learned that Enron declared bankruptcy and underwent one of the largest reorganizations in US history. This came as a direct result of "accounting loopholes, special purpose entities, and poor financial reporting" (*Wikipedia* 2021). Even without the nudging in this conversation's prompt, this appears very similar to the strategy of a Ponzi scheme. Enron executives were able to hide major losses from business dealings and presented the company as healthy and thriving to investors and the public alike. This bears a striking resemblance to a Ponzi scheme operator hiding losses to convince the next flight of investors to cough up their dollars. After the Enron bubble burst, their stock price plummeted from over $90 a share all the way down to less than $1. After all was said and done, their bankruptcy was the largest in United States history

L. W. Lee and A. Keathley, *45 Conversations About Behavioral Economics*, https://doi.org/10.1007/978-3-031-05046-6_35

up to that point. The head executives at Enron were indicted, charged, and in some cases jailed for crimes like obstructing justice and destroying documents.

The Enron scandal is similar to a Ponzi scheme in how the investors fared. Once a Ponzi scheme is reaching the end of its life span, the promises to investors tend to get fanatical and outrageous. This is the last desperate attempt to gain new investors and this class of investor loses the most. Early investors have a chance to get their money back, but each step down the pyramid, the returns become less and less as assets get stretched thinner and thinner and things unravel. Similarly, the Enron investors received very little back. Those few that got anything back got it through lawsuits (Wikipedia).

Overall, the Enron scandal shows me how firm managers of large firms can easily blur the lines between legal and illegal activities. It is very interesting to think about Ponzi scheme as an inherent part of firms.

Lee: Ponzi scheme and Enron scheme are equally bad frauds. Yet most of us see Enron as the lesser of two frauds. A large firm produces a lot of things. Some are good things such as wealth, jobs, choices, and innovation. Some are bad things such as injustice, envy, deception, fraud, crime, manipulation, trickery, and pollution. Yes, most of us are quick to extol the good things, skimping over the bad things and the ugly things. We all wear blinders.

When we get into the bowel of a firm, we will always find Ponzi schemes. Remember our conversation about a firm manager's obsession with growth? To impress others, the manager wants to make the firm grow and grow, in whatever ways and directions. How to pay for the mergers, acquisitions, new employees and plants? Find money in whichever ways possible: equity, short-term bond, long-term bond, bank loans, you name it. Because the aim is growth per se, it does not matter if growth is profitable or not. To cover up the trail (rather, entrails), the manager will think and act exactly like Charles Ponzi. What is more, the firm's legal status serves as another cover. Complex accounting makes it possible for one part of the firm to siphon off money from other parts. It is money laundering, none the less.

Akerlof and Shiller are two rare economists who see deception and manipulation lurking in any organization. If we don't see them, that is because we turn a blind eye on them. The willful blindness is "sloppy and wrong-minded" (Akerlof and Shiller 2015, p. 164).

Now that I have got your attention, I want to make one more point about scamming and then call it a conversation. (I am running a little Ponzi scheme for attention here!) Scammers are not just private agents. The biggest scammers are governments. A government collects taxes as payment for public goods and services, but it does not always deliver as promised. A government has the power to tax Peter to pay Paul. Of course, governments get scammed, too. Rich people can evade taxes by setting up shell companies, exploiting loopholes, sending lobbyists, and otherwise cheating money in ways you and I cannot imagine.

References

Akerlof, George A., and Robert J. Shiller. *Phishing for Phools: The Economics of Manipulation and Deception*, Princeton University Press, Princeton, 2015.

Wikipedia. "Enron Scandal." *Wikimedia Foundation*, 15 January 2021: https://en.wikipedia.org/wiki/Enron_scandal.

Further Reading

Akerlof, George A., and Robert J. Shiller. *Phishing for Phools: The Economics of Manipulation and Deception*, Princeton University Press, Princeton, 2015.

Creative Destructors: Tesla and Impossible Burger

Prompt Make a case for Tesla as a creative destructor. If you prefer, do Impossible Burger. In either case, tell us what it creates and what it destroys.

Keathley: Creative destruction is a natural phenomenon in market-based economies: new firms and industries making old firms and industries obsolete by innovation. Today, creative destruction is evident in the technology market. For example, consider the smartphone in your pocket. This product could not exist without the flip phone coming first. Nokia, the Apple before Apple existed, no longer exists because new firms innovated, and Nokia became obsolete. Another example is the infamous collapse of Myspace. Just like with smartphones, a new firm improved drastically on the product that previously dominated the market. Myspace had once completely owned the social media market, until Facebook took the successful aspects of Myspace and fine-tuned them to create Facebook. The old firm could not compete and soon became insolvent. Many think that the next major act of creative destruction would be with Tesla in the automobile market.

As many citizens search for ways to reduce their impact on the environment, automobiles have been placed under extreme scrutiny. Consumers are demanding energy efficient cars and green ways to power these new machines. According to a Bloomberg graph, last year electric car sales grew by 60% and by the year 2022 electric cars will cost the same as their

L. W. Lee and A. Keathley, *45 Conversations About Behavioral Economics*, https://doi.org/10.1007/978-3-031-05046-6_36

combustion engine counterparts (Randall 2021). And Tesla has been the top electric automaker by many measures (Furr and Dyer 2020). The Tesla Model S can currently go up to 410 miles on a single charge, which is farther than some cars can go on a full tank of gasoline (Tesla website). CEO Elon Musk hopes that soon they will be able to release a car that can go 1000 miles on a single charge.

The rise of electric vehicles will cause the decline of cars powered by combustion engines and gasoline. According to Carlier (2021), US car sales in 2019 were the lowest in 5 years and the 3rd lowest since 2005.

Gasoline cars are still the most common on the road, but that is slowly changing. If the big 3 auto makers do not adjust and try to transition to the electric car market, they will be destroyed. There currently is very little competition in the American market for electric vehicles. If Tesla is able to make their cars, charging stations, and solar panels affordable to the average American, the Big 3 will turn into the Big 1.

Lee: I have no interest in cars anymore, but I am fascinated with vegans. So I have been watching the food scene more than the car scene. In July 2019, I finally had my first Impossible Burger. It tasted fine. But it cost $16 plus change. I thought that its price would need to come down quite a bit to sustain this creative destructor. McDonald's, Burger King, and Wendy have taken notice, too. They are testing and selling burgers made of lab-grown or plant-based beef, chicken, and fish.

References

Carlier, Mathilde. "Vehicle Sales in the United States 1976–2020." *Statista*, 4 August 2021: https://www.statista.com/statistics/199983/us-vehicle-sales-since-1951/.

Furr, Nathan, and Jeff Dyer. "Lessons from Tesla's Approach to Innovation." *Harvard Business Review*, 18 February 2020: https://hbr.org/2020/02/lessons-from-teslas-approach-to-innovation.

Randall, Tom. "Here's How Electric Cars Will Cause the Next Oil Crisis." *Institute of Energy (IENE)*, 25 February 2021: https://www.iene.eu/heres-how-electric-cars-will-cause-the-next-oil-crisis-p3240.html.

Tesla. "Model S." accessed on 29 August 2021: www.tesla.com/models.

Further Readings

Lee, Li Way. "Franchising and Interbrand Competition." *Southern Economic Journal,* July 1984, pp. 219–234.

Perry, Mark. "The 'Amazon Effect' Is Creative Destruction at Its Finest." *Foundation for Economic Education*, 20 March 2017: https://fee.org/articles/the-amazon-effect-is-creative-destruction-at-its-finest/.

Creative Destructors: Creative Destruction Everywhere

Prompt Look for creative destruction in the following three markets:

a. banking
b. energy
c. retail

In each, what is being created and what is being destroyed?

Keathley: Normally I would look up an article and learn about the topic before forming an opinion, but I think I am qualified to opine about creative destruction in banking. I think so because my generation and people even younger are changing the way we as a society interact with money and with each other. Five years ago, if I helped out a friend or family member to the extent that I was going to get paid, the go to method was cash. That has changed due to the advent of apps on smartphones. From my phone, I can pay my credit card bill, send friend money for giving me a ride, and invest in the stock market. These are all things that used to require a physical bank branch or an ATM. In the coming years, I expect my generation's use of apps to deal with finance will only grow, and the people around us will have to adapt to it. Cash is no longer king.

To illustrate this, let me tell a brief story. The other day I was in my living room talking to my mom about her daily errands and whatnot.

L. W. Lee and A. Keathley, *45 Conversations About Behavioral Economics*, https://doi.org/10.1007/978-3-031-05046-6_37

She mentioned that she had to buy tickets for my sister's softball team banquet, but she could not think of a way to fit driving across town to the person collecting the money into her busy day. I, being the creative destructor that I am, said "why don't you just Venmo" her? "Ven-what?" she replied. I laughed because what was commonplace for people my age was completely foreign to her. However, after a 10 minute explanation and download, her tickets were purchased. I have been sent money on Venmo by my mom many times since. In your free time, take a look at PayPal's stock price (they own Venmo). I think "Venmoing" is here to stay.

In the previous conversation, we discussed Tesla as a creative destroyer in cars. Tesla, I think, is also a creative destructor in energy. Besides electric cars, Tesla has also ventured into the solar panel and battery market. It has improved on the design of solar panels, along with developing newer and better batteries, to be installed in the home. Instead of marketing toward the environmental crowd, Tesla makes its products appeal to the wealthy yet conscientious consumers. It highlights the environmental benefits yes, but it focuses more on how its products save money in the long run. Their home charging stations and solar panels are more of an optional feature to Tesla cars than a completely different product. Making these devices more efficient and making them mainstream has paid dividends for Tesla. Aside from the physical improvements to these devices, Tesla's advertising strategy also qualifies it as a creative destructor in marketing.

My first thought about creative destruction in retail stores was that retail stores appear to be dying out. Now more than ever during the Covid-19 pandemic, consumers want to make purchases online and have products delivered to them. We see this in the explosion of online shopping and the closure of brick and mortar stores. Grocery stores, as retailers, are not being spared. Through apps, major groceries stores allow you to have your items picked and pre-paid. You can simply drive up and have your items loaded up in your car and go. This is about safety and convenience. Consumers are willing to pay a premium for the arrangement. An extra kicker is that these services are often free when purchase exceeds certain threshold. Grocery stores also are developing ways to make the checkout portion of the transaction faster for in-person shoppers. Lately, at Sam's Club stores, my mom has used the "scan and go" feature. You do the work of the cashier; you scan your items on your phone as you shop and pay with a credit card. Once you are done, you

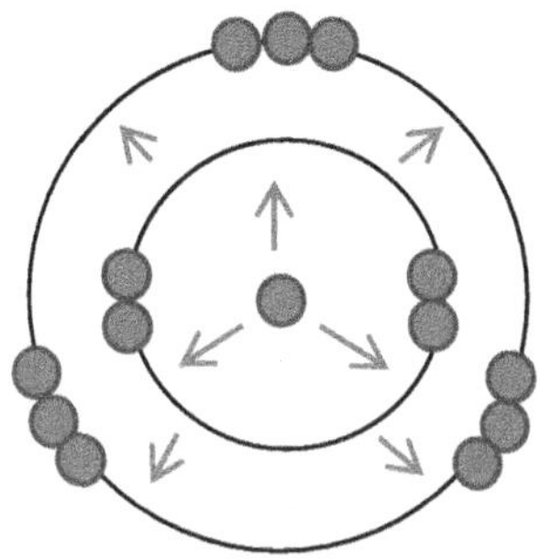

Fig. 37.1 Creative destruction in vaccines

hit the "complete" button, your card is charged, and you walk right out of the store. So I think grocery stores are right in the midst of waves of creative destruction in retail.

Lee: You have a sharp eye for creative destruction.

I have noticed that, when we talk about creative destruction, we don't make references to supply and demand curves anymore. But I like to picture creative destruction. Imagine that, over five years, we have taken three snapshots of the market for coronavirus vaccines. The snapshots are superimposed to yield Fig. 37.1.

- snapshot 1: In the beginning, there is only one vaccine. It is at the center of the picture.
- snapshot 2: There are two vaccines, each being produced by two firms. The market is the inner ring in the picture.
- snapshot 3: There are three vaccines, each being produced by three firms. The market is the outer ring of the picture.

Two things are going on here: There are more varieties over time, and within each variety there is more competition. Both are good for consumers.

You may be wondering what has happened to the first blockbuster vaccine. Well, it may have been replaced by late comers, or it may have survived as one of the nine vaccines in the picture.

This brings me back to your story about banking apps. You use several apps, but not cryptocurrency. We need to keep an eye on it. Cryptocurrency being currency, it threatens a central bank's reason for existence. The US central bank is considering its own cryptocurrency now (Lipton and Livni 2021). Meanwhile, El Salvador has taken the lead by adopting Bitcoin as legal tender (Lopez and Livni 2021). As Joseph Schumpeter (1950, p. 84) would say, cryptocurrency is a "gale of creative destruction."

References

Lipton, Eric, and Ephrat Livni. "Crypto's Rapid Move Into Banking Elicits Alarm in Washington." *The New York Times*, 5 September 2021: https://www.nytimes.com/2021/09/05/us/politics/cryptocurrency-banking-regulation.html.

Lopez, Oscar, and Ephrat Livni, "In Global First, El Salvador Adopts Bitcoin as Currency." *The New York Times*, 7 September 2021: https://www.nytimes.com/2021/09/07/world/americas/el-salvador-bitcoin.html.

Schumpeter, Joseph A. *Capitalism, Socialism and Democracy*, 3rd edition, Harper & Row, New York, 1950.

Further Reading

Lee, Li Way. *Industrial Organization: Minds, Bodies, and Epidemics*, Palgrave Macmillan, Switzerland, 2019.

Raiders: Your Favorite Corporate Raider

Prompt Look up a few "famous corporate raiders." Talk about one who jumps out at you.

Keathley: To understand corporate raiding, I read about Carl Icahn in the Wikipedia article. Icahn is a most famous corporate raider. He started off as a stockbroker at The New York Stock Exchange. In 1978, he began his career in raiding. His first big success was the hostile takeover of Trans World Airlines (TWA). He purchased a majority of the TWA stock, and he did this through what is called a leveraged buyout. This means he bought out the shareholders by using borrowed money. Once Icahn did this, he took the company private, and in 1988 he began a process called asset stripping. This is a tactic in corporate raiding where the firm's assets are sold to pay for the loan taken out for the leveraged buyout. Icahn did this by selling the London routes that TWA owned to American Airlines for $445 million (Wikipedia).

Directly after this and other cost cutting measures, TWA underwent two bankruptcies in the late 80s and early 90s. Once everything was all said and done, Icahn netted a profit of $469 million, while leaving the firm with a debt of $540 million. After Icahn left, TWA experienced more of the hardships his management caused by going through one last bankruptcy before being bought and then dissolved in 2001 by American Airlines (Wikipedia).

L. W. Lee and A. Keathley, *45 Conversations About Behavioral Economics*, https://doi.org/10.1007/978-3-031-05046-6_38

After TWA, Icahn would continue to target hundreds of firms in the following decades. He held two million shares of Genesis Intermedia, he was the second largest shareholder in the video game firm Take-Two Interactive, he owned 33.5 million shares of Motorola, and he had stock in lots of other firms across the tech and biotech industries. Notable other firms that he once held stock in or was on the board of are Blockbuster Videos, Marvel Comics, Netflix, Apple, Dell, Lyft, Xerox, Pep Boys and Lionsgate Films. He also joined the Donald Trump Administration as an economic advisor and financial regulation advisor. He worked on cutting environmental regulations for several energy firms that he held majority stock in (Wikipedia). He left this position in 2017 only after a possible conflict of interest came to light.

In my personal opinion, it is people like Icahn that make us skeptical of big business and of Wall Street. Throughout the article, I saw a constant theme: he enters a company, he does some financial maneuvering, he leaves, and the company goes under or never recovers. I think that corporate raiders as a whole are not a good thing for the economy. They seem to be all about consolidating wealth, no matter who it hurts or impacts. In case you could not tell, after reading about Icahn, I have very few nice things to say. Obviously, business will never be fun, friendly, compassionate, or fair, but something about using your wealth to essentially sink another firm for a profit sickens me.

Lee: I can tell that you are not fond of corporate raiders, to put it mildly.

I have a different take on corporate raiders. I see corporate raiders as part of the ecology of a market. Just as there are bacteria in a digestion system, there are corporate raiders in a market system. (Some bacteria are even probiotic.) In any case, corporate raiders keep managers on their toes. That is a good thing.

Keathley: Could you elaborate on why corporate raiders are a good thing and not a detriment to the economy?

Lee: Surely. Raiders are people who have a good sense of smell of open wounds. If a firm is bleeding, raiders will be attracted to them. And if the wounds are big and bloody, raiders will come knocking to offer fixes. They will want to do one of three things:

1. Take over the firm and fire the manager - unless the manager pays ransom money.
2. Take over the board of directors, patch up the open wounds, and resell the firm for capital gains.
3. Take over the firm, break it up into parts, and sell off the parts. The sum of the values of the parts can be greater than the value of the whole broken thing.

These venues for raiders are possible only if the managers are pursuing self-interest instead of owners' interest. This is why I think corporate raiders are the Ninjas and Vikings in the economy. They keep bad managers awake at night. They don't bother good managers.

Anyhow, independent raiders like Icahn are an endangered species in the market ecosystem. Raiders are forming groups and rebranding themselves as investment firms. When a "private equity firm" rep knocks on your door, watch out.

Reference

Wikipedia. "Carl Icahn." *Wikimedia Foundation*, 2 November 2020: https://en.wikipedia.org/wiki/Carl_Icahn.

Further Readings

Gaughan, Patrick. *Mergers, Acquisitions, and Corporate Restructurings*, 6th edition, Wiley, Hoboken, NJ, 2015.

Lee, Li Way. *Industrial Organization: Minds, Bodies, and Epidemics*, Palgrave Macmillan, Switzerland, 2019.

CONVERSATION 39

Raiders: Four Defenses Against Raiders

Prompt Corporate managers have four defenses against raiders:

a. greenmail
b. golden parachute
c. poison pill
d. Pacman

How do they work?

Keathley: Greenmail works like ransom. A target company may ask to buy the raider's shares of the company stock at a premium. Greenmail is the portion of the payment over and above the market value of the shares. "After accepting the greenmail payment, the raider generally agrees to discontinue the takeover and not buy any more shares for a specific time" (Hayes 2020a). Essentially, a corporate manager uses this technique to buy time. This technique reminds me very much of Somali pirates. They would take over a cargo ship until they were ransomed away.

Hayes (2020b) also describes what a golden parachute is. He defines it as "substantial benefits given to top executives if the company is taken over by another firm, and the executives are terminated as a result of the merger or takeover." While this seems like CEOs getting severance deals with cushy benefits, it serves as a powerful anti-takeover technique. If raiders know that when they takeover this firm, they will be on the hook

L. W. Lee and A. Keathley, *45 Conversations About Behavioral Economics*, https://doi.org/10.1007/978-3-031-05046-6_39

for these massive severance packages, they may give up. Golden parachute is a win–win for the executives.

Managers use poison pills to discourage raiders. There are two kinds: "flip in poison pill" and "flip over poison pill" (Hayes 2020). The former is a provision whereby shareholders are presented with the option to buy more shares at a heavily discounted rate once the raider hits a certain threshold of ownership, say 40%. This would cause the raider's shares to be diluted and the acquisition to become much more expensive. The "flip over poison pill" is a provision that entitles shareholders to purchase a stock at a discounted rate. However, the stock this time is that of the raider's firm. This can scare off raiders fearful of dilution of their own company. Poison pills have been used lately by Papa John's to prevent an ousted founder from becoming a majority owner, and by Netflix, which aimed to prevent Carl Icahn from taking over the firm (Hayes).

Lastly, to understand the Pacman defense, I turned to Daniel Liberto (2020). He defines it as a "defense tactic that involves the target company attempting to acquire control of the company that bid for it by purchasing large amounts of its stock." The firm that is under siege by a raider uses the firm's cash to make a play at acquiring the raider's firm. They do this hoping they either will take over the raider's firm and profit from it or scare the raider off. This is a very high-risk maneuver because if the firm using the Pacman defense actually acquires the raider's firm, it likely will be overleveraged in the short term.

Lee: I can tell that you are feeling uneasy about the whole conversation: you avoid pointing your finger at the manager. I had the same feeling of cognitive dissonance when I first learned of corporate raids. On one hand, I felt sorry for the manager. On the other hand, I felt flabbergasted to learn that the manager under attack can defend by using shareholders' money. I did not find these raiders and managers in textbooks.

Keathley: Are there any risks to going private? Why do more companies not stay private if the risk of raiding is so high?

Lee: Going private runs the risk of limiting access to capital, hence growth. A manager does not like that. Going private also runs the risk of limiting the separation of ownership and control. A manager does not like that, either.

References

Hayes, Adam. "How Greenmail Works." *Investopedia*, 4 September 2020a: www.investopedia.com/terms/g/greenmail.asp.

Hayes, Adam. "Golden Parachute Definition." *Investopedia*, 29 August 2020b: www.investopedia.com/terms/g/goldenparachute.asp.

Hayes, Adam. "Poison Pill Definition." *Investopedia*, 22 September 2020c: www.investopedia.com/terms/p/poisonpill.asp.

Liberto, Daniel. "Pac-Man." *Investopedia*, 24 September 2020: www.investopedia.com/terms/p/pacman.asp.

Further Reading

Gaughan, Patrick. *Mergers, Acquisitions, and Corporate Restructurings*, 6th edition, John Wiley & Sons, Inc., Hoboken, New Jersey, 2015.

PART IV

Happiness

We all devote ourselves to the pursuit of happiness. Only in recent years have behavioral economists and psychologists begun to find out how successful we are in the pursuit.

The answers are all over the map. Still, they strongly suggest that happiness depends on a couple of things in the market system:

A. Income
B. Justice

(We have 6 conversations about happiness.)

Much is at stake here. If life in a system is not the happiest possible, then people should get out of the system. (Remember Karl Marx?) But how do we get out and where do we go after we get out?

Income: Inequality USA

Prompt Look up income inequality in USA. What are your concerns about it?

Keathley: My first concern is that the gap between the highest earners and the lowest earners is continuing to widen, with no end in sight. According to David Leonhardt and Yarnya Serkez (2020), the GDP of the United States since 1980 has risen 79%, but the income of the bottom half of earners has only gone up by 20%. If wealth consolidation at the top continues at this pace, how long will it be before the bottom half of earners in the world's richest country are impoverished?

My second biggest concern is that the middle class is not doing much better. According to the same article, the middle (top 50–90%) earners have only gone up by 40% since 1980. At this point, we are talking about a wealth gap that encompasses 90% of income earners in the nation. That is a super majority of Americans. One cannot write off 90% of the population as freeloaders, bums, lazy, or any of the other derogatory terms that get thrown around to describe those who are struggling to make ends meet.

My third biggest concern is that the top 10% of earners are gaining wealth so rapidly that it resembles a late stage game of monopoly rather than a working economy. The top 10% of earners have seen their incomes increase by an astounding 420% since 1980 (Leonhardt and Serkez 2020). The rich are getting richer and the poor are getting poorer. That is a

L. W. Lee and A. Keathley, *45 Conversations About Behavioral Economics*, https://doi.org/10.1007/978-3-031-05046-6_40

Fig. 40.1 The corruption-inequality loop

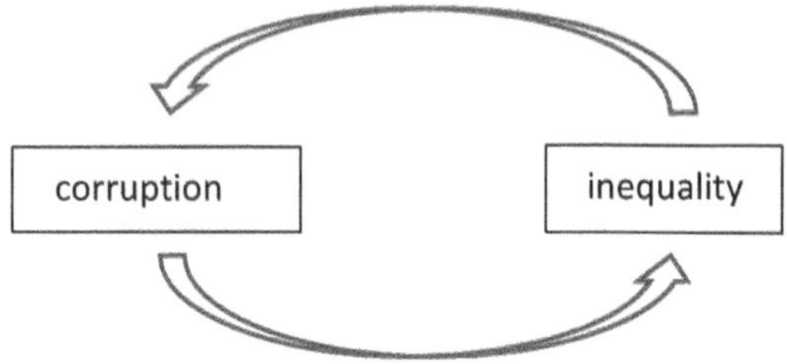

common political cliché, but clichés do not appear from nowhere. It is simply a fact that income inequality exists and is growing.

My fourth concern is that the problem is getting worse. The many social programs, subsidies, or other things that aimed to help solve this problem have not worked. Political pundits spend hours talking about how millennials are "the entitlement generation," meaning that young people are always looking for handouts. However, I would call young people "the coin-flip generation." I say this because a graph in the Leonhardt and Serkez article shows that a person born after 1980 has 50% chance to be making more than their parents. This compares with 92% in the 1940s.

After reading this article, I am more concerned about the humanitarian consequences of income inequality. For example, the richest Americans live on average 13 years longer (Leonhardt and Serkez 2020). That is a huge difference as lifespan goes.

I do not mean to turn this conversation into one about politics, but our elected officials are a reflection of those that elected them. In 2021, a majority of voters did not cast their ballots with income inequality in mind. With a government so highly divided, I cannot see major changes in income inequality in the near future.

Lee: I am with you. The other day, I read about billionaires (Manjoo 2020). There are more than 600 billionaires in the U.S. now. Their number is growing. Their average wealth is also growing. Can you fathom a number like $6 billion? I can't.

It does not bother me a whole lot that billionaires wear more diamonds, play with bitcoins, and live longer lives. What bothers me most is their greater ability to corrupt. Corruption feeds inequality. Figure 40.1 describes what I see: a feedback loop between corruption and inequality.

Why do corruption and inequality matter, though? Well, they make up unhappy. Corruption makes us distrust each other, and inequality makes us feel insecure. When we distrust each other and feel insecure, we are unhappy. Let's talk about this next.

References

Leonhardt, David, and Yaryna Serkez. "America Will Struggle After Coronavirus. These Charts Show Why." *The New York Times*, 10 April 2020: www.nytimes.com/interactive/2020/04/10/opinion/coronavirus-us-economy-inequality.html?action=click.

Manjoo, Farhad. "Even in a Pandemic, the Billionaires Are Winning." *The New York Times*, 25 November 2020: https://www.nytimes.com/2020/11/25/opinion/coronavirus-billionaires.html?action=click&module=Opinion&pgtype=Homepage.

Further Readings

Ferreira, Francisco H. G. "Inequality in the Time of Covid-19." *International Monetary Fund*, Summer 2021: https://www.imf.org/external/pubs/ft/fandd/2021/06/inequality-and-covid-19-ferreira.htm.

Stiglitz, Joseph E. *The Price of Inequality: How Today's Divided Society Endangers Our Future*, W. W. Norton & Company, New York, New York, 2012.

Income: Easterlin Paradox

Prompt There are surveys of "life satisfaction" across countries. There is a puzzle in the surveys. Take, for example, two small groups: (a) Denmark, U.S., France and (b) Costa Rica, New Zealand, Switzerland. In both groups, income seems to make no difference to life satisfaction. What is going on?

Keathley: I looked up a figure in Altman (2012, p. 303) and extracted from it the two groups in the prompt. Figure 41.1 shows them side by side.

First, we will look at the group on the left: Denmark, U.S. and France. These are all developed nations and have similar GDP per capita levels. The differences come in their happiness levels. These countries are wildly apart on that axis. Denmark is by far the happiest of the three, while France is the least happy of the three. In the middle is U.S. The relationship among these three countries suggests that money is not a very good predictor of happiness.

Now we turn to the group on the right: Costa Rica, New Zealand, and Switzerland. They report very similar happiness levels but have very different GDP levels. This data would go to show that happiness and income are not linked because despite having less money a Costa Rican is just as happy as any Swiss person.

Figure 41.1 shows no causal relationship between GDP per capita and happiness. I need to delve deeper into the literature. I am curious as to

L. W. Lee and A. Keathley, *45 Conversations About Behavioral Economics*, https://doi.org/10.1007/978-3-031-05046-6_41

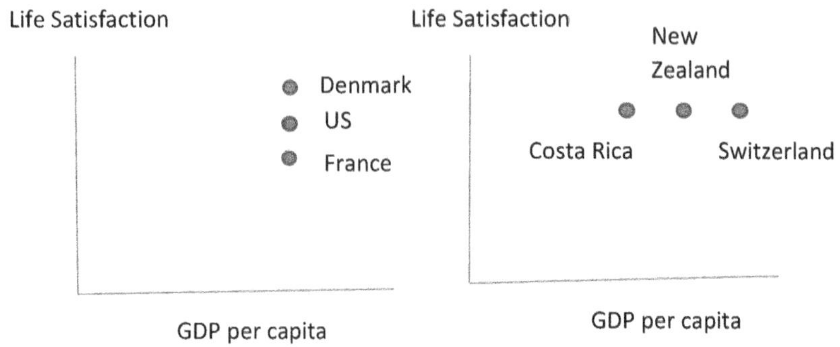

Fig. 41.1 Life satisfaction and income: two views

how life satisfaction is defined. Every language has a different word for life satisfaction and each country has a different culture. Perhaps the word for happy in Thai has a connotation of arrogance so people refuse to call themselves such. Or maybe Japanese feel societal pressure to report being happy. Happiness is subjective; everyone defines it differently.

I think the pictures in Fig. 41.1 show that happiness depends on more than the average income of a group. Let's suppose that 5 people were surveyed in France and Denmark each. Imagine that the incomes in France were: $10, $10, $20, $100, $120 and the incomes in Denmark were: $74, $70, $60, $84, $72. The GDP per capita is $72 for both groups. However, there is more income inequality in the France group than in the Denmark group. Perhaps the citizens of Denmark are much happier because the average Dane lives on an income much closer to the mean than the average Frenchmen does. In other words, maybe the relationship between income and happiness relies more on relative income position than solely on average income.

Lee: All your questions about how to define and measure happiness make sense. Indeed they are known collectively as the Easterlin Paradox, which has been driving the research on happiness. It is funny that, after one hundred years of chasing economic growth for the sake of happiness, we are finding that we have been chasing the rainbow.

Keathley: Yes, it is. So far, what are their solutions? We hear a lot from politicians but not a lot from economists.

Lee: Psychologists already know that the single-minded pursuit of income does not make us happier. But economists have a hard time saying they know as well. "Hey, folks, take it easy. Our job is to make a bigger pie. We don't know why you are not happier about a bigger pie."

Something else about the literature on happiness bothers me even more. You see, the GDP per capital in those surveys does not include Nature (i.e., air, water, climate, etc.). Yet, all over this planet, income has been growing at the expense of Nature. As we now realize, Nature is fundamentally a type of capital in production. (Without Nature, we would produce exactly nothing.) So, when measuring income generated by using Nature, we need to treat the decline in Nature as a cost and subtract it from income. That is just proper accounting practice. When we do that properly, there is little net income growth left. Partha Dasgupta (2007) thinks that some economies have not grown for decades, because they pollute (or get polluted) so much.

When Nature is taken into account in GDP per capita, the life satisfaction chart may look different. I am very curious if someone has done such a chart.

Keathley: I wish cable news talked about this side of economics as much as they talked about GDP, unemployment, and inflation.

References

Altman, Morris. *Behavioral Economics for Dummies*, John Wiley & Sons Canada, 2012.

Dasgupta, Partha. *Economics: A Very Short Introduction*, Oxford University Press, New York, 2007.

Further Readings

Frey, Bruno S. *Happiness: A Revolution in Economics*, The MIT Press, Cambridge, Massachusetts, 2008.

Our World in Data. "Self-Reported Life Satisfaction Versus GDP Per Capita," accessed on 29 August 2021: https://ourworldindata.org/grapher/gdp-vs-happiness.

Income: Hedonic Treadmill

Prompt On an exercise treadmill, we work hard and go nowhere. That is an intended consequence. On a hedonic treadmill, we work hard and get no more happiness. That is an unintended consequence. But we have two options:

A. Any of us can jump off the hedonic treadmill.
B. Together we can turn off the hedonic treadmill.

Let's talk about what would happen to your happiness if you do A, and then if we all do B.

Keathley: If only I get off the hedonic treadmill, I believe that I will suffer tremendously. I no longer will be making as much money. Sure I am eliminating the pain from running to keep up with others on the treadmill, but at what cost? Assuming that my jumping off point will be at a place where I can support my material needs, I will, in theory, not lose any quality of life. I will still be able to enjoy the things I currently enjoy and live the quality life that I currently live. However, American culture is built on the principle of excesses, not the principle of sufficiency.

Our culture and our society look favorably on those who have all of their needs met and yet find ways to purchase new things. If I jump off and others in my reference group continue on the hedonic treadmill, I will be looked down upon. I believe that this will make me less happy. This

L. W. Lee and A. Keathley, *45 Conversations About Behavioral Economics*, https://doi.org/10.1007/978-3-031-05046-6_42

goes back to the findings of the happiness research that we just talked about. The only moment of redemption in this is when those on the treadmill hurt themselves and descend down the treadmill to take their licks. For this brief moment I may feel better off because it is better to not gain than it is to lose. Our good old friend loss aversion is back at it.

In the scenario that the entire society jumps off the treadmill, I imagine that happiness will also be quite low initially. People no longer will have all the things that they had before. However, in the long run, relativity in wealth kicks in again. People will find joy in the fact that they all are in the same boat. This is when the culture will change. The culture will shift from one of excess to one of sufficiency. No longer would people compete to outdo each other on their credit card bills. Rather, everyone would come to appreciate living within their means and not trying to outdo each other. If everyone's wealth and happiness is stagnant, there is no reason to try to get ahead. This society sounds like something that Karl Marx would approve.

Overall I think both of these scenarios are quite unrealistic. I don't know how one could jump off this metaphorical treadmill, or how an entire society could jump off it. Assuming that society did jump off the treadmill, what would stop some from jumping back on? In the current world, we all choose to keep running on the treadmill and trying to race the person next to us.

Lee: I share your trepidations about jumping off the hedonic treadmill, all by yourself or with others. After all these years of trying myself, I still have at least one leg on the hedonic treadmill most of the time. I have not become a recluse or a revolutionary yet.

The tricky thing about happiness is that it depends so much on one's reference group and one's relative position in the reference group. Figure 42.1 shows you what I mean.

Here is a story about a hedonic treadmill with two runners. Suppose Jim and Mike are coworkers in the mailroom. They form a reference group. Jim has been happy because his income is higher than Mike's by 5%. Then, one day, Mike gets a 10% raise, while Jim gets a 2% raise. That puts Mike ahead of Jim on the hedonic treadmill. How does Jim feel now? Happier because his income is higher? Or unhappy because his income is now lower than Mike's? Call the emotion jealousy or envy or vanity. It is what powers the treadmill.

We all are pursuing happiness, but few of us know what happiness is and how elusive it is. We know more today, thanks to scientists who are

Fig. 42.1 A hedonic treadmill

not afraid of asking big questions. By the way, we will soon talk about if animals run on hedonic treadmills, too.

We do know that happiness depends on many things: relative position, Nature, public goods, quality of institutions, trust, health, etc. As you point out, happiness also depends on culture. If the treadmill is to stop and everyone is to get off, culture will have to change first. How? That is the question that Karl Marx and Mao Zedong asked. They thought they knew how.

Further Readings

Craig, Heather. "45 Best Happiness Books and Are They Worth Your Time?" *Positive Psychology*, 12 February 2021: https://positivepsychology.com/best-happiness-books/.

Frank, Robert H. *Choosing the Right Pond: Human Behavior and the Quest for Status*, Oxford University Press, New York, NY, 1985.

Frank, Robert H. *Luxury Fever*, The Free Press, New York, NY, 1999.

Gentry, W. Doyle. *Happiness for Dummies*, John Wiley & Sons, 2008.

Pennock, Seph Fontane. "The Hedonic Treadmill—Are We Forever Chasing Rainbow?" *Positive Psychology*, 4 July 2021: https://positivepsychology.com/hedonic-treadmill/.

CONVERSATION 43

Justice: Capuchin Justice

Prompt Justice is a pillar of happiness, and that is not just a human quirk. How do capuchins feel about justice? What can we learn from them?

Keathley: Experiments show that monkeys care about justice. Stokes (2014) and Kristof (2017) describe an experiment in which monkeys retrieve a pebble and are rewarded with a cucumber slice. The interesting bit occurs when one monkey sees the other getting a better reward. When a monkey saw the other getting a grape rather than a cucumber slice for the same task, that monkey threw away the cucumber slice in anger.

Humans are very much the same. As a college student I have a lot to say about tuition costs and things of that nature, and people always respond by saying: "that is not fair." They say that I should be mad at those who have inferior grades and yet pay the same or less tuition than I. These people have the same mentality as that of the monkeys. In my opinion, we should not always ask if something is fair nor not. Rather, we should ask if something makes society better off as a whole. When I tell these people that I would not mind in the slightest if someone gets a similar or better scholarship package than me because of things other than merit, they are bewildered to say the least. The way that I see it, the more people are able to go to college, the better off our country is. I do not want to see anyone be denied access to higher education solely because they cannot afford it. If colleges had been tuition free, I still would have tried just as hard to get good grades in high school, I still would have

L. W. Lee and A. Keathley, *45 Conversations About Behavioral Economics*, https://doi.org/10.1007/978-3-031-05046-6_43

applied for private scholarships, and I would have been just as happy for others as I would for myself.

When we act like the monkeys, we are really saying: "I do not care how much I benefit from the system. If I benefit less than others, I want to get rid of the whole system." Often fairness should be a consideration when making public policy, but fairness alone should not determine if a program live or die.

Lee: I understand your sentiments here, but I am afraid that you are pretty much in the minority. Out of ten people, there may be one who feels like you about justice. The other nine will be outraged like the monkeys when they are not treated fairly. In a political system where people's feelings carry equal weights, they are nine times as important as you are. So if they see a public policy proposal as unfair, they are going to vote it down, and you can't say they are wrong.

Economists must take monkeys seriously. Setting up a hypothetical welfare function and maximizing it by calculus does not do anyone any good. Economists must spend more time looking at the real world. In the real world, people are not that different from monkeys. Instead of throwing grapes and cucumbers around, people throw rocks and fire bombs. A recent incident as such was the "Yellow-Vest Protests" over fuel tax in France (Wikipedia).

Another question occurred to me when you were describing the experiments. In one experiment, there are two capuchins, one getting grapes and one getting cucumber slices. I wonder what they would do if they saw a third capuchin getting a cinnamon bun. (Monkeys love junk food, too!)

Keathley: I would imagine that the cucumber and grape monkeys would get angry (cucumber monkey being the angrier) because they both just moved down a peg in their reference group.

Lee: Another question. The list of justices is long: there are food justice, water justice, air justice, racial justice, age justice, employment justice, housing justice, income justice, etc. Why are economists so slow in doing something about them?

Keathley: I would say because it is hard. For everything humans know about math and rocket physics we still cannot figure out how to be fair with one another. I think humans have trouble understanding things that cannot be expressed empirically or mathematically.

References

Kristof, Nicholas. "What Monkeys Can Teach Us About Fairness." *The New York Times*, 3 June 2017: www.nytimes.com/2017/06/03/opinion/sunday/what-monkeys-can-teach-us-about-fairness.html.

Stokes, Stephannie. "Why Monkeys Care About Fairness and What It Means for Us." *WABE*, 12 November 2014: https://www.wabe.org/why-monkeys-care-about-fairness-and-what-it-means-us/.

Wikipedia. "Yellow Vests Protests," accessed on 14 September 2021: https://en.wikipedia.org/wiki/Yellow_vests_protests.

Further Readings

Lee, Li Way. *Behavioral Economics and Bioethics*, Palgrave Macmillan, Switzerland, 2018.

Verdolin, Jennifer. "Why Does Fairness Matter?" *Psychology Today*, 16 March 2018: https://www.psychologytoday.com/us/blog/wild-connections/201803/why-does-fairness-matter.

Justice: Utilitarian and Pareto Principles

Prompt What is justice? It is hard to have agreement on justice about a fixed system. It is a little easier to have agreement on justice about a change in a system. Take a population of two persons: Rich and Poor. Say Rich makes \$8 and Poor \$2. Then suppose a policy change takes place, with the result that Rich makes \$15 and Poor makes \$5. Is the policy change just? Let's make use of two principles. The *Utilitarian Principle* says that a change is just if and only if the change benefits the greatest number of people. The *Pareto Principle* says that a change is just if and only if it makes at least one person better off, and nobody worse off. What do you think?

Keathley: Under the Utilitarian Principle, I would say that the policy change is neither just nor unjust. There are only two persons in the population, and the policy change does not benefit anyone else. It does not matter how the increase in wealth got distributed between Rich and Poor. If the policy change results in the appearance of a third person getting a slice of the income pie, then the story will be different.

Under the Pareto Principle, I would say that the policy is just. In the example, both Rich and Poor have more income after the policy. End of proof. Under the Pareto Principle, it does not matter if the gain is big or not. What matters is that no one loses from a change in the economy.

L. W. Lee and A. Keathley, *45 Conversations About Behavioral Economics*, https://doi.org/10.1007/978-3-031-05046-6_44

I would like to discuss the Pareto Principle with its advocates and see if they consider the effect of hedonic treadmill. A policy change may benefit one so much more that it changes their relative positions on the treadmill. As we talked about earlier, that will make someone happier and the other unhappier than before the change.

Lee: Great thoughts. Let me add a bit more fodder for thoughts here. Have you heard of the Rawlsian Principle? It is named after John Rawls, a philosopher. It says that a policy change is just only if it increases the happiness of the unhappiest person in the reference group. By extension, a policy is *optimal* only if it *maximizes* the happiness of the unhappiest person in the reference group. In our example, the policy change does not go far enough according to the Rawlsian Principle. Unless there is some limit to how much change can be made, the $20 of new level of aggregate ought to be allocated to Poor until Poor has the same level of income as Rich. That means equal distribution of income.

The differences among the Utilitarian Principle, the Pareto Principle, and the Rawlsian Principle boil down to two assumptions about happiness: (i) measurability and (ii) comparability.

Utilitarian Principle assumes:

i. A person's happiness is measurable.
ii. Two persons' happinesses are comparable.

Pareto Principle assumes:

i. A person's happiness is measurable.

Rawlsian Principle assumes:

ii. Two persons' happinesses are comparable.

Are you still with me? I like the Rawlsian Principle best. I bet the monkeys also like it best.

Further Readings

Britton-Purdy, Jedediah. "What John Rawls Missed." *The New Republic*, 29 October 2019: https://newrepublic.com/article/155294/john-rawls-missed-create-just-society.

Rawls, John. *A Theory of Justice*, Belknap Press, Cambridge, Massachusetts, 1971.

Sen, Amartya. *The Idea of Justice*, Allen Lane, London, 2009.

CONVERSATION 45

Justice: Gross National Happiness

Prompt The Kingdom of Bhutan has a constitution that specifically promotes Gross National Happiness (GNH). That is unique. Are people there happier than people in the U.S.?

Keathley: I read an article by McCarthy (2018) to learn what GNH is about. GNH came about as a way to implement the ideals of the nation's religion, Buddhism. Some such ideals are "compassion, contentment, and calmness."

I noticed that Bhutan wasn't a particularly happy nation. McCarthy (2018) reports: "When the United Nations released a report ranking countries by happiness last year, Bhutan was nowhere near the top. Norway took the crown. The U.S. ranked 14th. Beautiful Bhutan came 97th." The article goes on to talk about the double digit unemployment numbers that are increasing, especially among the nation's young workers. In 2016 the number was up to 13.2%. Other problems they face are underdevelopment, a small economy, climate change, and energy. Compared with developed nations, Bhutan appears to have done better on one front: It has not had any military conflicts in 50 years.

My biggest takeaway from this article was that, as always, life is complicated. Most Bhutan residents reported being at least somewhat happy; only 10% reported being less than "narrowly happy." I would attribute the majority's happiness to their public goods, such as free healthcare, free utilities, lack of international conflict, and simple routine lives. In the

L. W. Lee and A. Keathley, *45 Conversations About Behavioral Economics*, https://doi.org/10.1007/978-3-031-05046-6_45

U.S., people enjoy none of these public goods. However, the U.S. is rated much higher on the UN's happiness index. (I guess UN's happiness index is much less comprehensive than Bhutan's own happiness index.)

This illustrates, again, that happiness depends on many things in complex ways. Happiness depends on how it is measured, who is being asked, living conditions, social support, and so on. This is not a newsflash to anyone who has followed our earlier conversations.

I think much more research needs to be done on the Scandinavian countries. They show up in survey after survey as the happiest countries. What are they doing that we and the people of Bhutan aren't?

Lee: About the Scandinavian countries, everybody is asking the same question as you are asking. See the report on Finland by Hetter (2020).

Before this conversation, I knew little about Bhutan. So it came as a big surprise that Bhutan has happiness in its constitution. In doing this, Bhutan had no one to follow; it had to lead. Even among countries that practice Buddhism, Bhutan stands out for embracing happiness so openly and explicitly.

In a report on Bhutan, LaMotte (2019) quotes Bhutan's Prime Minister Lotay: "When we say Gross National Happiness, it is not the celebrative 'Ha ha – Ho ho' kind of happiness that we look for in life....It only means contentment, control of your mind, control of wants in your life....Our king rightly calls Gross National Happiness as development with values."

Lotay must know that Bhutan is climbing a mountain. It is not close to the peak yet. The path is steep and slippery. There are lots of bumps and holes along the way. Also, Bhutan's every move draws attention by foreigners who do not share its culture and values. Still, Bhutan is on the right path. For example, it is centuries ahead of western countries in its protection of environment. LaMotte (2019) observes: "The country has long partnered with the World Wildlife Fund to protect native wildlife in numerous parks. Plastic bags have been banned since 1999. Tobacco has been banned since 2005, making Bhutan the world's first smoke-free nation. The Bhutanese constitution mandates that at least 60% of the country remain under forest cover."

That shows me that, in the pursuit of happiness, Bhutan is the visionary.

Keathley: Do you think that there is any hope for Western Europe or the United States to take anything from Bhutan and implement it? Or are these nations, the U.S. in particular, too individualistic?

Lee: I think that Western Europe and U.S. are beginning to follow Bhutan. However, they are nudging each other on a grand hedonic treadmill, not seriously climbing the mountain toward Gross National Happiness.

References

Hetter, Katia. "During a Pandemic, What Does Being the World's Happiest Country Mean?" *CNN*, 20 March 2020: https://www.cnn.com/travel/article/worlds-happiest-country-wellness-2020/index.html.

LaMotte, Sandee. "Meet the Smoking-Free, Carbon-Negative Country That Passes No Law Unless It Improves Citizen's Well-Being." *CNN*, 13 September 2019: https://www.cnn.com/2019/09/13/health/bhutan-gross-national-happiness-wellness/index.html.

McCarthy, Julie. "The Birthplace Of 'Gross National Happiness' Is Growing A Bit Cynical." *NPR*, 12 February 2018: https://www.npr.org/sections/parallels/2018/02/12/584481047/the-birthplace-of-gross-national-happiness-is-growing-a-bit-cynical.

Further Readings

OPHI. "Bhutan's Gross National Happiness Index." *Oxford Poverty & Human Development Initiative*, accessed on 21 August 2021: https://ophi.org.uk/policy/gross-national-happiness-index/.

Schumacher, E.F. *Small Is Beautiful: Economics as If People Mattered*, Harper & Row Publishers, NY, 1973.

Manning, John. "The Limitations of GDP as a Gauge of Nations' Well-being." *International Bankers*, 1 July 2021: https://internationalbanker.com/finance/the-limitations-of-gdp-as-a-gauge-of-nations-wellbeing/.

Afterword

This book is our record of what we see when we take disciplinary blinders off. We can't say that we have taken all the blinders off, as we don't even know how many we had on when we started the conversations. But we can say that we just see so much more.

L. W. Lee and A. Keathley, *45 Conversations About Behavioral Economics*, https://doi.org/10.1007/978-3-031-05046-6

Index

L. W. Lee and A. Keathley, *45 Conversations About Behavioral Economics*, https://doi.org/10.1007/978-3-031-05046-6

The manufacturer's authorised representative in the EU is Springer Nature Customer Service Centre GmbH, Europaplatz 3, 69115 Heidelberg, Germany. If you have any concerns regarding our products, please contact ProductSafety@springernature.com

Printed and bound by CPI Group (UK) Ltd, Croydon, CR0 4YY
30/09/2026
02225327-0001